THE
BASEMENT
BOOK

THE BASEMENT BOOK

By
Harris
Mitchell

New Trend
New York · Toronto · Munich

Published by
New Trend Publishers
31 Portland Street
Toronto, Ontario   M5V 2V9

Technical Consultant:. Al Burnes

A New Trend Book
New York, Toronto, Munich

Distributed in the United States by
Dodd, Mead & Company
79 Madison Avenue
New York, N.Y. 10016

Library of Congress Catalog Card Number: 83-062510

Canadian Cataloging in Publication Data

Mitchell, Harris
   The Basement Book
Includes index.
ISBN 0-88639-010-9

1. Basements.   2. Basements—Remodeling.   I. Title.
TH 3999.M57 1983   643'.5   C83-099031-3

Printed and bound in Canada by John Deyell Company

Introduction

If you want to gain confidence and experience in home improvement work, there is no better place to start than in your own basement. Many thousands of homeowners have learned the basics of house construction, carpentry, wiring, plumbing and a number of other trades just by building a recreation room in an unfinished basement.

The basement offers many advantages as a training school for home handymen; for example, it's always warm and convenient—just a few steps from your living room. Even if you only have an hour to spare in an evening, you can slip down there and get something important done, and leave it ready to be continued the next time you have a break.

It's out of the way. You can make a mess down there for months without upsetting the rest of the house or interfering with normal household activities. And when you make mistakes, as you certainly will, you're the only one who needs to know about it.

The difficulty of the work progresses as you learn. It starts off easy and gets trickier as you go along, which is the best way to learn anything. The first rough framing is impressive but fairly simple, and it will soon be covered up, anyway. The more demanding finishing and cabinet work come later, when you've gained confidence and don't mind spending more time to do a better job. This is where the amateur often does better work than the professional, although it may take him five times as long to do it.

But don't be impatient. I've discovered that there are two kinds of home handyman. One wants to do the work as fast as he can and can't wait to get it finished. He has only one satisfaction—the completed job. The other takes pleasure from each step, each achievement, each problem solved. His satisfaction is in the continuing process of building and learning new skills, and his only disappointment comes when the job is finished.

There's no question about which is better off, and I can only hope that everyone who uses this book will relax and enjoy each step in the process of transforming an unfinished basement into an attractive and useful living area.

Contents

1 Recreation Room Ideas

With finished floor space in a house now worth around $30 a square foot, it doesn't make much sense to use all that warm, dry, space in the basement as a storehouse for cast-off toys, clothes, furniture and other household effects on their way to the junk pile.

Admittedly every house needs storage space for garden furniture, luggage, out-of-season sports equipment and other flotsam and jetsam of modern living. But even allowing for that, as well as the furnace room and laundry area, you still have space for finished rooms that can add 25% to the usable floor area of your house ... at one-tenth the cost.

The nice thing about building a new living area in the basement is that it doesn't have to match the rest of the house. It can be anything you want — a book-lined hideaway, an English pub, a secluded den, a family room, a hobby area, a playroom for the children or an entertainment area where you and your friends can relax and have fun without worrying about the furniture.

The old idea of a rec room has fallen into disfavor. This was usually little more than a long, narrow, cold room, poorly lit and completely empty except for a small bar counter in one corner. If it contained any furniture at all, it was something that had been banished from upstairs. The only time the rec room looked attractive was when it was full of people. The rest of the time it was about as inviting as a deserted army barrack.

The trend today is to turn that wasted basement space into a finished and furnished living area that is as attractive and comfortable as the rest of the house, but a lot more interesting. Don't underestimate your ability to do it. A square box may seem like the simplest design, but more complicated floor plans with angles, alcoves, built-ins, raised floors, dropped ceilings and an imaginative decorating scheme are not that much harder to build ... they just take a little longer. Some of the finest and most elaborate finished basements in the country were built by amateurs who learned each step as they were taking it, but were not afraid to try.

The possibilities are endless, as you can see by the examples shown on the following pages. But every house has its own structural limitations, and every family has its own requirements and tastes, so it's not expected that you will want to duplicate any of the rooms shown here and we make no attempt to give you detailed construction plans. We hope that they will give you some good ideas, however, and inspire you to develop designs and variations of your own.

The elegant accents of ornamental ironwork and Roman blinds are combined with the rustic mood of barnboard and old brick in this basement room in the home of interior decorator Burt Manion. The fake fire-hood was made of galvanized sheet metal, hammered and painted black.

John and Linda Tolhurst gained extra width in their basement family room by hiding the steel supporting posts (above) inside the decorative partition walls at either end of the chesterfield alcove seen in the photograph on the right. The lower edge of the main beam was taken as the level of the recessed ceiling, with dimmer-controlled fluorescent lights hidden behind the edge. The ceiling is gypsumboard with a textured paint finish.

Recreation Room Ideas

Preparing a Plan

The design of your recreation room or other basement living area will depend partly on the nature and location of such obstacles as the furnace, oil tank, water heater, laundry tubs, drain pipes, windows, back door, and structural members like the main beam·and its supporting posts. You will have to leave storage space for garden furniture, storm windows, bicycles, and other bulky, but essential, household possessions. And you must be careful not to block access to important maintenance points such as the electric service panel, water meter and shut-off valve, and drain clean-out plugs.

When you have determined the general area that is available to work in, draw a simple floor plan to scale, marking in all the items that must be accommodated. Use an 18″ x 22″ pad of ¼″ or ½″ squared paper and draw your floor plan at a scale of ½″ to 1″, then add the walls (actual or projected) folded down as shown in the illustration on the right.

If you get a pad of tracing paper that's the same size, you can slip your floor-and-wall plan under a sheet of the translucent paper and sketch or doodle various floor layouts on it without marking up the original plan.

The position of the stairway will help to determine how the space can best be used. You will generally have more usable floor area to work with, for instance, if the stairs are at one end of the basement rather than in the centre, as they sometimes are. Enclosed stairwells that take a right-angle turn at a mid-point landing are particularly awkward because they make it very difficult to get sheets of plywood and similar materials downstairs. Shown below are a few of the floor plans that can be achieved with different stairway locations.

Left — The use of rounded, Fancy-Butt shingles and louvred shutter panels has added interesting textures to this basement room. Turned balustrade and pillar salvaged from an old house add to the Gay Nineties atmosphere that the pink and white color scheme seems to suggest.

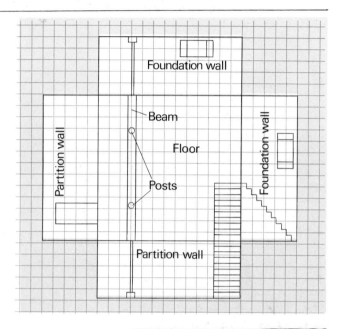

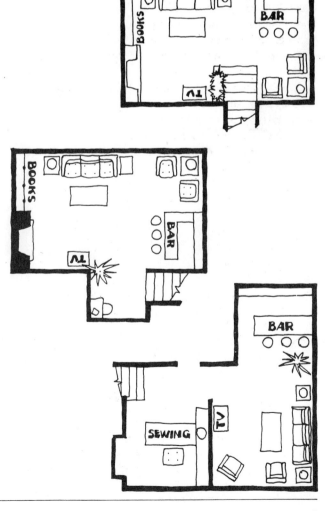

2 Wet Basements

There are two very different causes for damp basements. One is condensation on the cold concrete, which generally occurs during the summer when the humidity is high and the basement is cooler than the rest of the house because it is below ground level. This type of dampness can be cured by insulating the walls or by using a dehumidifier.

The other cause of wet basements is outside moisture getting through the concrete walls or floor. This is the one that causes most of the trouble, and it must be remedied before the basement can be finished, otherwise mildew, wood decay and peeling paint will ruin your work.

Another test for dampness is to fasten a 12" square of polyethylene film to the concrete with masking tape. If moisture forms under the film in a few days, seepage is the problem. If moisture collects on the room side of the film, it is caused by condensation.

Of course, these tests only show the condition at the time the test is made. Basement dampness is usually a seasonal problem. And often there is no need to test; the water can be seen leaking through cracks or holes in the wall.

Repairing Cracks and Holes

Cracks most commonly appear in the mortar joints of concrete block walls, but they also occur in poured concrete walls, usually at weak points such as in the corner of window openings, or where there is a change in the height of a foundation wall. Such cracks may be caused by earth settlement or natural shrinkage of the concrete.

Cracks can be patched over on the inside, but the best place to repair them is on the outside of the wall.

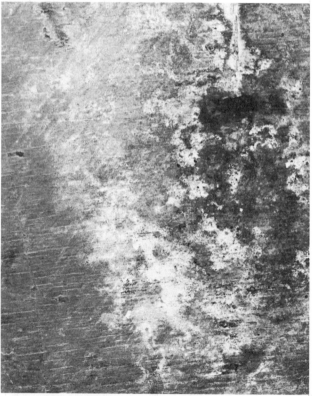

It isn't difficult to tell whether basement moisture is caused by condensation or seepage. The appearance of a white, fluffy powder on the surface of the concrete is a sure sign that moisture is coming through it. This "efflorescence" consists of mineral salts that have been leached out of the concrete and left on the surface when the water evaporates. The concrete may appear dry, but the efflorescence proves that it isn't.

Dig down to the bottom of the crack and remove all loose concrete and dirt. Wet the crack thoroughly, then fill it with one of the many latex-cement patching materials available at hardware stores and building supply dealers. Also available are prepared caulking compounds made for use on concrete, as shown above.

Immediately cover this with a 6″ wide strip of fibreglass roofing tape or with strips of fibreglass window screen to reinforce the patch.

After the crack-filler has set, brush on a coat of fibrated asphalt roof patching compound, about 6″ on either side of the crack.

Brush on another coat of fibrated asphalt and let this dry for 2 or 3 days before back-filling the hole — carefully, to avoid damaging the patch.

Wet Basements

Leaks

Leaks are sometimes found where holes have been left by concrete form ties ... the wires or rods that hold the wood forms together while the concrete is setting. While these should also be patched from the outside in the same way that a crack is done (see previous page), they can sometimes be filled and sealed from the inside with a plug of fast-setting hydraulic cement that expands as it hardens. Quick Plug and Set Plug are two common brands.

These materials can even be applied while the hole is actively leaking. Before the hole is filled, however, it should be chiseled out about 1½″ deep and undercut at the bottom to lock in the plug. If the hole is dry, it should be moistened thoroughly before patching

The hydraulic cement powder is mixed with enough water to produce a putty consistency. Since it begins to set in 2 or 3 minutes, only a small quantity should be mixed at one time. The putty is formed into a cone shape, with the base of the cone about 1″ larger than the diameter of the hole. As soon as the hydraulic cement cone begins to feel warm it is rammed into the hole and held there firmly with the palm of the hand for about 5 minutes, long enough for it to expand and set in the hole. If necessary, top off the hole with a trowelled coat of hydraulic cement.

Drainage

After cracks and holes have been filled, you will have to remedy the basic cause of the trouble: inadequate drainage around the foundation footings. Even if the foundation shell (concrete walls and floor) were completely waterproof, the buildup of water outside the basement could cause serious damage, exerting enough pressure to crack the walls and lift the floor. (If the water outside the foundation walls is just 12″ above the floor level, it will exert a pressure of more than 30 tons under a 1,000-square-foot floor.)

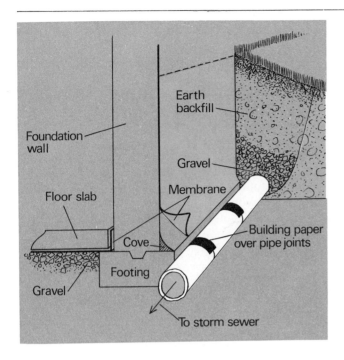

Heavy storms can bring more water than the drain tiles can handle. Roof runoff is often a source of trouble. In areas where the soil is sandy enough to provide good drainage, down-spouts can be connected to the drainage system around the foundation footings. But in many parts of Canada this is not permitted, and it is necessary to direct down-spouts away from the house with a diversion pipe or a concrete splash pad.

A down-spout should never be allowed to discharge directly on to the ground beside the basement wall.

Window wells can also cause water problems if they are not connected to the foundation drainage system.

Sometimes the drainage system may fail after a few years because fine soil has sifted in and blocked the tiles. This is often due to the use of insufficient gravel when the tile bed was laid. Experts now recommend that the tile be covered with 18″ of crushed stone or gravel. Where the subsoil is silt or fine clay, it may even be advisable to add a layer of coarse sand or other granular back-fill to within 12″ or 18″ of the ground surface.

Concrete block walls are more likely to crack than poured concrete. They also tend to be more porous. And since the blocks are hollow, water can run down inside the wall and build up pressure at the bottom.

Building codes require that a drainage system be laid around the base of the foundation walls and connected to the local storm sewer or sanitary sewer. This should be capable of draining ground water away from the house to prevent a buildup of water pressure against the walls and under the floor. But a number of things can go wrong.

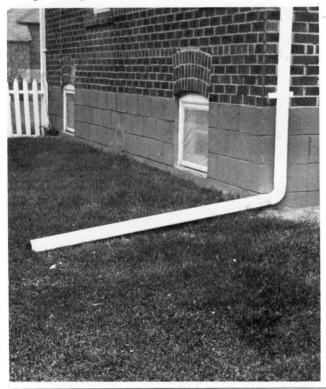

The planting of deep-rooted and water-hungry trees, such as willows, near the house frequently leads to blockage of the drain tile system by a mass of fine roots. Other than removing the offending tree, root pruning is the only way to prevent this trouble. This can be done by digging a trench between the tree and the house and cutting off all the roots encountered. They will grow again, of course, so this job must be done every few years.

Once the roots have blocked the drain tiles, the only remedy is to dig down and clean them out or replace them. Mechanical drain cleaners won't work in this type of tile, and there are no chemicals that are effective in removing the roots.

Wet Basements

Blocked drainage can also be caused by careless back-filling when the house was built, which can dislodge or break the tile. Again, the only remedy is to dig down and repair the damage. The location of the trouble can often be determined by the area of dampness on the concrete wall, but waterproofing contractors sometimes locate a blocked drain tile by injecting a dye into the tile bed at selected locations and watching for it to appear in the floor clean-out trap.

Basement drainage problems are sometimes caused when the owner of an old house with a shallow basement decides to lower the floor to make more headroom. If the new floor is below the level of the foundation footings, there will be no way to get rid of water under the slab other than a sump pump. And even this will not work if the floor is below the water table.

Surface Drainage

Recent studies have indicated that poor surface drainage is the major cause of wet basements. The earth that is replaced in back-filling around the foundation wall often settles enough to form a depression that directs surface water toward the house and down the outside of the foundation wall. The simple remedy in this case is to build the earth up around the house so that surface water will run away from it.

Poor sitting and grading of subdivisions is another common cause of drainage problems. If your house has a wet basement and your neighbors' houses do not, it may be because you're getting the runoff from their property. One remedy is to re-grade your lot to divert the flow of water around your house.

Drainage Repairs

In most cases, however, faulty or inadequate drainage around the foundations is the cause of a wet basement. The best remedy is to dig down to the bottom of the foundation wall, clean or replace the drain tile, and check the run to the sewer main to make sure this is clear.

While the foundation wall is exposed, all cracks and holes should be filled as described on Page 19. The entire wall should then be coated with fibrated asphalt foundation compound. If the concrete seems porous, it may be advisable to apply a waterproof membrane, such as a sheet of 4-mil polyethylene film or over-lapping layers of glass-felt roofing paper (see illustration Page 21).

This is unquestionably the best way to cure a wet basement, but it's a lot of work if you do it yourself, and expensive if you have it done by a contractor. Contractors charge from $25 to $50 a running foot, which can mean several thousand dollars for a moderate-sized home. Fortunately, there are alternatives.

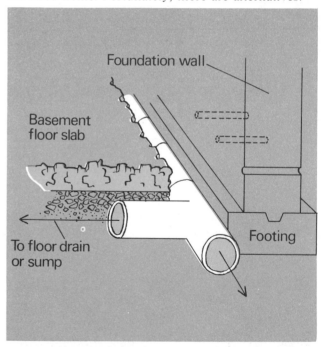

Inside Drainage

Where it is impractical or impossible to excavate to the foundation footings outside the house (because of a driveway, perhaps) drain tile can be laid under the basement floor, inside the house.

A narrow trench is broken through the concrete floor and dug down to the bottom of the footings.

Holes are drilled in the bottom of the foundation wall to relieve the water pressure outside. Drain tile (flexible, perforated, plastic pipe is used here) is laid in the ditch and connected to the existing floor drain or to a sump, where it can be pumped away. The tile is covered with fine gravel and then topped with concrete to the original floor level.

Pressure Treatment

A number of basement waterproofing contractors offer a "no digging" remedy that involves pushing pipes down the outside of the foundation wall and pumping in a liquid that will flow along the wall and seal the leak.

The liquid is generally a solution of bentonite, a fine, colloidal clay that is widely used to seal oil wells and artificial lakes. Bentonite is a good waterproofing material, but there is some question about how effective it, or any other chemical, can be when applied to the outside of a concrete wall several feet below the ground by this method. There is also the problem of the bentonite plugging the weep holes in the drainage system around the footings.

Nozzles have been designed to reduce these problems, but it is difficult for the home-owner to know what is being used or how well the job is being done. As with most other home improvement trades, a great deal depends on who does the work.

In the hands of an expert who understands drainage problems, knows what remedy to apply where, and who stands behind his work, the pressure application of bentonite can be an effective and economical way to cure some wet basements. But usually it is only part of the answer ... drainage must still be provided, cracks must be sealed from the inside with epoxy cement, mortar joints re-pointed, and poor surface drainage corrected.

Wet Basements

Waterproofing Paints

Good concrete is virtually waterproof but the mix and methods sometimes used in house foundations, particularly old ones, can produce a concrete that is quite porous. Even a moderate amount of moisture in the soil can cause dampness and efflorescence on the inside walls.

As we have seen, the best place to waterproof such a wall is on the outside, but there are some things that can be done on the inside. The traditional treatment is to brush on two or more coats of plain portland cement powder and water. White portland cement is generally used, and is the basis of most powdered waterproofing paints. This treatment will fill and seal surface pores and hold back a certain amount of seepage.

The development of a new family of butadiene resins related to synthetic rubber, unaffected by the alkali in concrete, has led to the production of premixed, solvent-based waterproofing paints. Unlike the water-mixed paints, however, these cannot be applied to a damp wall, which may present some problems.

There are a number of brands of concrete waterproofing paint on the market, both powders and premixed that can cure some seepage problems, but adequate drainage around the foundation footings is still essential to prevent a buildup of water pressure that can crack a concrete floor slab.

Cracks and open mortar joints are chiseled out and undercut so that the patching cement will hold firmly.

Hydraulic patching cement is pressed into the open cracks and the floor joint is coved for greater strength.

A coat of waterproofing paint is applied to the dampened patches after they have set. The paint should be mixed stiff enough to support a brush, as shown below.

Two coats of thick waterproofing paint are applied. The first one is brushed into the surface very carefully, to fill all voids and hairline cracks.

Waterproofing Contractors

There are many firms in the basement waterproofing business, and most of them are conscientious and reliable. The Better Business Bureau and government consumer protection offices across the country report very few complaints in this field.

But there are many possible causes and cures for a damp basement, and not every repair is going to be 100% successful. It may be many months before the home-owner finds out, so it is important to deal with a company that will stand behind its work.

The best way to find a reliable contractor — perhaps the only way — is on the recommendation of satisfied customers. Any firm that has been in business for a number of years should be able to give you the names and addresses of other people in the area for whom they have done work. Don't be afraid to contact them. Better still, ask if you can drop in and see what was done.

Check the firm's place of business and find out how long they've been there. Ask the Better Business Bureau and your provincial consumer protection department if there have been any complaints against the company.

A reliable contractor will charge nothing for examining your problem, suggesting a treatment, and giving you a firm, written price quotation. Get bids from two or three companies. But remember, the low bid may not be the best.

Pay or sign nothing until you have seen a written contract that states exactly what is to be done, what materials are to be used, when the job is to be started and completed, what guarantee is given, and what the price will be. The contract should cover "repair and waterproofing", otherwise you may find yourself charged for essential repair work that was not included in the contract.

Waterproofing contractors generally give a warranty of some kind, but it may not be as good as it sounds. Some only guarantee to carry out a certain operation, such as laying new drain tile or applying a coating to the wall. They don't guarantee that this treatment will cure the problem.

Other guarantees have a clause saying that if the treatment you have paid for doesn't work, the company will come back and do something else — *for which you must also pay.* A good guarantee will give a 5-year protection against any further seepage in the area treated, and provide all additional repair work required, at no extra cost.

Don't be misled by claims that the company or the salesman is bonded. That may only mean that the firm has a "license bond" required by the municipality, assuring that it abides by local building regulations. This has nothing to do with how well a particular job is done nor does it provide any guarantee of contract performance. A salesman's bond may be a similar license bond, or just a "fidelity bond" that protects his employer against possible theft of company property. Again it has nothing to do with guaranteeing the proper performance of your contract.

Contractors are generally required to give performance bonds for government work, and in this sense they may say that they are bonded, but such bonds are taken out on each individual contract and do not apply to other work done by the same company. Performance bonds are almost unknown in home repair work.

Be suspicious of a firm that wants a large deposit; well-established companies don't need one. However, a modest down payment of 10 – 20% at most — can be made when the contract is signed. In most provinces you also have the right, under the mechanics' lien act, to withhold 15% of the total bill for 40 days *after the job is completed.* This is meant to protect you against the contractor who hasn't paid his workers, but it will also give you a chance to make sure the work was done to your satisfaction.

3 Insulation

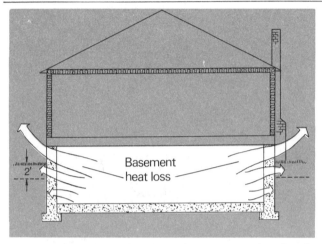

Basement
heat loss

2'

In an otherwise well-insulated house, an uninsulated basement can account for as much as 25% of the total heat loss. Most of this is lost through the walls above ground level, but there is some loss down to about 24″ below ground level.

There is, however, very little heat loss through any part of the wall, *or the floor*, below that level. This means that it doesn't pay to insulate a basement floor; the cost is far more than the saving, and the money spent on a built-up, insulated floor would be better spent on a good carpet, laid directly on the concrete.

Strictly speaking, the walls don't need to be insulated more than 24″ below ground level, but this only applies if the insulation is tight against the wall, for example where plastic foamboard is applied directly to the concrete with mastic adhesive, or where batt insulation between the studs fits tight against the foundation wall. Otherwise the cold air behind the insulation will drop down into the lower part of the wall (below, left).

Outside Insulation

In some situations it may be more convenient, and less expensive, to apply insulation to the *outside* of the foundation wall. (Some experts believe this reduces the chance of frost damage in areas where very low winter temperatures are experienced.) This is done by applying foamboard insulation — at least 2″ thick — to the foundation wall down to 18″ or more below ground level and then extending another slab of foamboard out horizontally, as illustrated here.

The vertical foamboard can be fastened directly to the concrete with mastic adhesive or gun-type

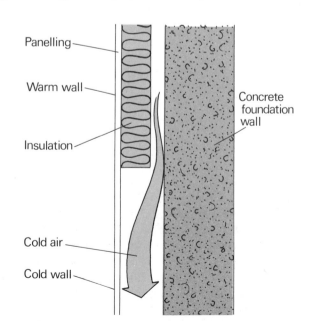

Panelling

Warm wall

Insulation

Concrete
foundation
wall

Cold air

Cold wall

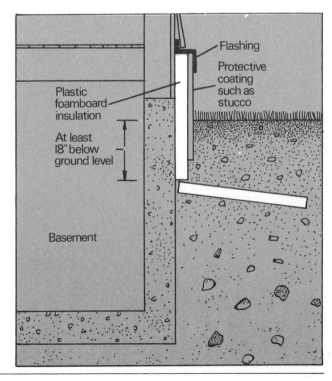

Flashing

Protective
coating
such as
stucco

Plastic
foamboard
insulation

At least
18″ below
ground level

Basement

fasteners.

To keep water from getting behind the insulation, the top should be covered with flashing extending up under the siding. Foamboard above the ground must be protected with asbestos-cement board or stucco. Ordinary stucco requires a supporting structure of wire screen or expanded metal, but this is not needed if you use a premixed acrylic-cement stucco. This can be painted with any exterior latex paint.

Kinds of Insulation

There are two kinds of insulation that can be used in basement walls: batts and foamboard. (Aluminum foil has very little insulation value in this application, and is no longer accepted under the Residential Standards of the National Building Code.)

The familiar fibreglass insulation batts are made of thin filaments of glass held together with a plastic binder. Less common now, but still cheaper, are mineral wool or rockwool batts made of blown filaments of steel mill slag, usually dark orange or brown in color.

Batts come in bundles of 48″ lengths or in 32′, 56′ and 80′ rolls. They are available in thicknesses of 2¾″ to 12″. Standard widths are 15″ and 23″ to fit between 16″ and 24″ stud spacing.

At one time almost all insulation batts came with a vapor-proof, kraft paper face with tabs on either side that were stapled over the studs. This doesn't provide a very good vapor barrier, however, and the preference today is to use the plain "friction fit" batts with no paper backing. These are simply pushed in place between the studs and then covered with polyethylene vapor barrier.

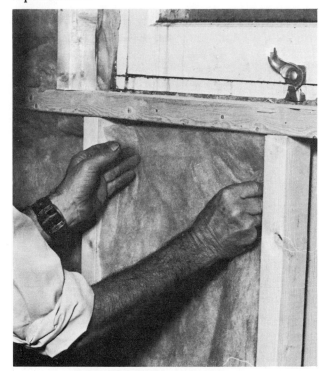

Batt insulation can be cut easily with a razor knife. If your hands are sensitive, you should wear gloves when handling this material.

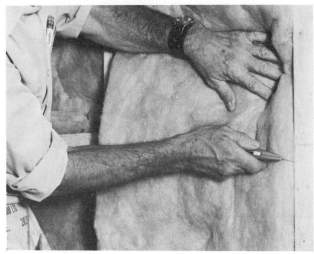

Foamboard

There are a number of different kinds of plastic foamboard insulation. Most common is the white, expanded polystyrene beadboard, so called because it is made of expanded pellets of styrene that resemble puffed rice. This material is often incorrectly referred to as Styrofoam, which is the Dow Chemical Company's trade name for a similar, but quite different, product.

Styrofoam is always blue in color. It is formed in a different manner, and has a higher insulation value — and price — than the common white beadboard. It is widely used in commercial construction, but is rarely seen at retail lumberyards or building supply dealers.

Polyurethane foamboard is the most effective insulation material available. It has almost twice the insulation value of the common white foamboard, but costs nearly five times as much and is not generally available on the retail market.

Insulation

Which Insulation Is Best?

Insulation was once commonly referred to in inches, but this is a poor way to measure it because some materials provide more insulation than others for a given thickness. The measurement that is now used is the Thermal Resistance Value, represented by the letter R. The higher the R number, the greater the insulation value. This is the number to check when you buy insulation, not the thickness.

The most important figure to consider is not the cost per inch of thickness, but the cost per unit (R) of insulation value. The accompanying tables give the R values for 1″ thickness of some common building and insulation materials, and the comparative cost on the basis of insulation value. (The metric measure for thermal resistance is RI, which is equal to R x .176. RI ÷ .176 = R).

As you can see by these tables, batt insulation is much more economical than even the cheapest of the foamboards. For most applications, it is also easier to use. The only place where foamboard is better than batts is for exterior use on concrete walls (see Page 26) and for interior application directly to concrete (Page 38).

How Much Insulation?

Canadian building codes now require basement walls to have an insulation value of at least R10. Since an 8″ concrete wall has an insulation value of about R2 (allowing .85 for the inside and outside surfaces) this means that you need to add at least another R6 in insulation.

You can achieve this with 1½″ of common white foamboard applied directly to the wall and covered with gypsumboard panelling (see pages 38-39). For about the same cost, however, you can get twice the insulation with a frame wall filled with 3½″, R12 batts. This is more work, certainly, but it is justified by the reduction in heating costs and the fact that it permits the use of a wider range of wall panelling materials and also provides a better surface for attaching cabinets, partitions, etc.

But it isn't enough just to put insulation between the studs; you must also plug those hidden spots where heat can be lost. Push strips of fibreglass between the rough frame and the window, around wiring and outlet boxes, behind drain and vent pipes. Be sure to place insulation along the inside of the end joist that sits on the foundation wall, and between the "headers," the ends of the joists that run at right angles to the foundation wall.

INSULATION VALUE PER INCH OF THICKNESS

Concrete	R 0.08
Plaster	R 0.17
Brick	R 0.42
Air space in wall	R 0.97
Wood	R 1.25
Vermiculite	R 2.08 - 2.5
Fibreglass batts	R 2.85 - 3.5
Mineral wool batts	R 3.33 - 3.7
Cellulose fibre	R 3.85 - 4.10
Plastic foamboard	
Common white	R 3.80
Styrofoam (blue)	R 5.00
Urethane	R 7.14

COST OF ONE SQUARE FOOT OF ONE UNIT (R) OF INSULATION
(Average retail prices, January 1982)

Cellulose fibre	1.6¢
Fibreglass batts	1.6¢
Vermiculite	4.9¢
Common white foamboard	5.5¢
Urethane foamboard	8¢
Styrofoam SM (blue)	8.4¢

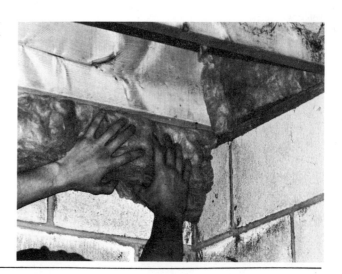

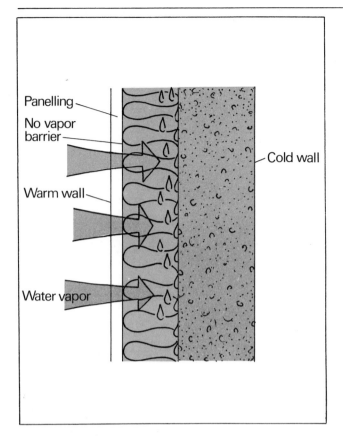

Panelling

No vapor barrier

Warm wall

Water vapor

Cold wall

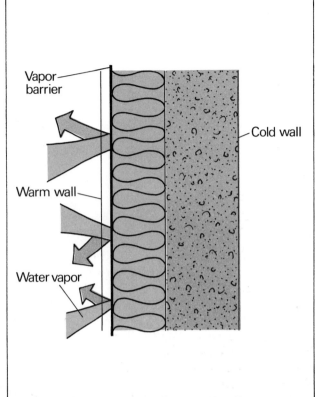

Vapor barrier

Warm wall

Water vapor

Cold wall

Vapor Barriers

There is a lot of confusion about the function of a vapor barrier. Many people think that the vapor barrier should be applied to the concrete wall to keep moisture out of the basement. That isn't how it works.

A vapor barrier is there to keep household moisture *inside* — to prevent warm, moist, household air from passing through the wall panelling into the insulation, where it would, at some point, be cooled enough to condense the way it does on a cold window. This would wet the insulation, soak through the wall, and eventually cause mildew and decay problems.

To prevent this from happening, a vapor barrier is placed *on the warm side of the insulation.* To be effective, it should provide an unbroken, impermeable membrane over the entire wall surface. Even small holes or open seams can permit enough moisture to get inside the wall to cause serious condensation problems. This is why the overlapping paper tabs on kraft-faced batts don't make a good vapor barrier.

Water vapor itself is not wet; it is simply a gas. But it is subject to a force called vapor pressure that tries to equalize the water vapor content between the two bodies of air that are separated by a porous material such as plaster, wood, brick, and even concrete. It can pass through materials that are impervious to water, such as paint. And vapor pressure is increased if there is also a temperature difference, as between the inside and the outside wall of a house.

The 2-mil thickness of polyethylene film is generally used as a vapor barrier. This is applied directly over the insulation, even if it already has a kraft paper, vapor barrier face. The film comes in rolls 100″ wide and 60′ long (500 square feet) but it is folded in two so that the top edge is stapled to the top wall plate with about 8″ overhanging the ceiling, then the sheet is unfolded down the wall and stapled to the bottom plate. The film should cover the window frames and extend around the wall so it can be overlapped in the corners to make an airtight seal. It should also extend over the ceiling and the floor, where it can be trimmed later.

A vapor barrier is only required over insulation, and is not needed, therefore, on a basement ceiling or floor. It is also not necessary over plastic foamboard insulation that is attached directly to the concrete, because this material is itself an adequate vapor barrier.

Panelling is applied on top of the vapor barrier.

4 Heating

A basement tends to be cooler than the rest of the house because the concrete walls and floor are below ground level. During the summer the temperature of the earth is much lower than the outside air. During the winter it is warmer than the outside air but still a lot colder than the air in your house, and the large mass of cold concrete enclosing the basement quickly absorbs the heat that is put into it.

This is why the basement always seems to get cold as soon as the heat goes off. But even when the air temperature in the basement is the same as upstairs, it tends to feel colder because body heat radiates toward the cold concrete.

All of these problems can be cured with adequate insulation (see Page 26). But if you have a warm air heating system there is another common cause of basement heating problems, and that is the lack of a cold air return vent off the basement floor. Basement heating outlets are usually located in the ceiling, and the warm air will stay up there unless the cold air is drawn off the floor and circulated through the heating system.

If the cold air return plenum enters the bottom of the furnace, it's a simple matter to insert a louvered grille where the cold air duct enters the furnace. A 6" x 10" sidewall return grille will usually be large enough to provide good, warm air circulation in the basement. Make sure the basement floor around the furnace is clean, otherwise the air drawn into this return grille will soon plug the filters. For best results the floor should be painted and then swept regularly.

If the basement living area is closed off from the furnace room it may be better to run a cold air return grille down inside an interior wall where it passes under the cold air return plenum in the ceiling, as shown in the illustration on the left.

If your present heating ducts are not in the right place to suit your finished room plan, they can be moved, shortened, or extended quite easily with pipes and fittings available at any building supply store. New ducts and registers can also be installed, but this will affect the balance of warm air distribution throughout the entire house and must be done carefully. In general, it's best not to add more than one new warm air register in the basement. Usually even this can be avoided simply by diverting an existing duct to serve the new location.

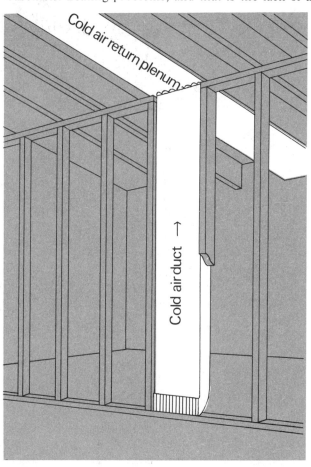

Cold air return plenum

Cold air duct →

After any changes have been made to the duct system, balance the heat flow by adjusting the dampers that are (or should be) located in each duct line close to where it takes off from the main heating plenum. The handle on the outside of the pipe indicates the position of the damper inside — parallel to the pipe, the damper is open; at right angles to the pipe, the damper is closed. If there are no dampers in the heating ducts you will have to adjust the air flow by means of the controls in the registers.

Auxiliary Heating

Your present heating system should have no trouble keeping a well-insulated basement as warm and comfortable as the rest of the house. As a matter of fact, the whole house will probably be warmer, and your fuel bills lower, after you have finished the basement.

Sometimes, however, additional heat is needed. If it is impossible, impractical, or too expensive to extend the existing heating system to take care of this, there are a number of ways that auxiliary heat can be provided.

Electric Baseboard Heaters are the most popular type of auxiliary heating for basements. Units are available up to 9' long for 120-volt and 240-volt wiring. Heat output is related to the wattage. A general rule is to provide from 6 to 10 watts of electric heat for each square foot of floor area.

The 120-volt units range from 500 watts to 1,500 watts. The 1,500-watt units require a separate house wiring circuit and are adequate for rooms up to 250 square feet in size. The 240-volt units go up to 3,000 watts, and one such unit can heat a room of up to 500 square feet, or about half the average basement. (In most cases, however, it would be better to use two or more smaller units on the same circuit.)

Electric baseboard units are individually controlled by built-in thermostats.

Gas-Fired Heaters may be less expensive to operate in some areas than electric heaters. Free-standing space heaters are available in sizes as small as 15,000 BTUs. Compact wall heaters that take up less than 10" of floor space are rated at 50,000 BTUs, enough to heat an entire basement living area. More decorative, perhaps, are the gas-fired, imitation fireplace heaters that hang on a wall or stand in a corner. These have a BTU rating of 25,000.

Although it is possible to vent some gas-fired auxiliary heaters through an outside wall or into an existing furnace flue, others must be vented straight up through the roof, which can be difficult and expensive in the case of a basement installation. Check the venting requirements carefully before buying a gas-fired heater.

Three different types of gas-fired auxiliary heaters are shown above — a free-standing space heater, a slim wall unit, and an imitation fireplace with realistic log flames.

Wood-Burning Stoves and Fireplaces are also popular as auxiliary heaters, although they can't maintain a constant temperature unattended.

5 Basic Tools

Nothing will do more to speed and simplify the work of finishing your basement — or any other home building project — than having the right tools. Shown opposite are most of the tools you will need ... all the essential ones, anyway. You may find you need other tools, such as a miter box and back saw, a staple gun, electrician's wire stripper, and drywall taping tools, but these are only needed for special work and are best left until you actually need them.

A word of warning: DON'T BUY CHEAP TOOLS. They are rarely worth the money.

Carpenter's Level This is used to determine if a stud is vertical or a countertop level. The longer it is the more accurate it is; 24″ is a good size for most work. Metal levels are more expensive than wooden ones, but never warp. Bubble tubes are set to read both horizontal and vertical levels.

Carpenter's Square Like the carpenter's level, the bigger this is the more accurate it is. A small combination square (see right) is used for marking lumber cut-offs, but a large steel carpenter's square, at least 24″ x 14″, has many uses in squaring a room, laying out floor tiles, checking corners, etc. Marked in inches, it can also be used to mark grades and pitches.

Claw Hammer This and a saw are the two tools you will use the most, so get one that will be easy to handle and give you good service. A 16-ounce hammer is best for most people, but if your wrist isn't too strong you'd be wise to choose a lighter one. Even two ounces makes quite a difference if you're doing a lot of nailing. Get one with an integral steel shaft and head and a moulded rubber grip. It's as strong as a crowbar and the head will never come loose.

Combination Square You will use this handy tool mainly for marking off lumber for right-angle cuts, but it is also designed to give 45° miter angles. The sliding, 12″ ruler can be locked in position to serve as a depth gauge or for marking lumber to a specific width. The cast-iron head contains a level, and there is usually a small awl in the end that can be used for marking lumber.

Crosscut Saw A good, general-purpose handsaw is essential. The blade should be 24″ or 26″ long, with 10 teeth to the inch (referred to as "10-point"), fine enough to give you a fairly smooth cut, and coarse enough to do it quickly. It can also be used for ripping or sawing with the grain.

Electric Drill A number of special features are worth looking for. Variable speed control is useful for starting holes, drilling concrete, and driving screws. A drill with a reversing switch can also be used for removing screws. Most drills will only take $\frac{1}{2}$″ bits; one with a $\frac{3}{8}$″ chuck is much more useful. And a plastic, "double insulated" housing is safer than the customary metal shell.

Jack Plane You'll need this to trim doors, plane lumber to size, shave the edge of plywood panels, and many other jobs. A 10″ plane is most convenient for general work.

Multi-Screwdriver You run into so many different kinds of screw heads these days — slotted, square, cross and variations of each in assorted sizes — that you need a toolbox full of screwdrivers to handle them all. Or a single multi-tool like this, the handle of which holds driver heads.

Nail Set Like most good tools, a nail set does something that nothing else will do as well — drive finishing nails below the surface without damaging the wood. The two most useful tip sizes for home carpentry are $\frac{1}{32}$″ and $\frac{1}{16}$″.

Plumb Bob and Chalk Line This handy tool combines two quite different functions. The chalk-filled case holds a reel of string. When stretched between two points along any surface, then snapped with your fingers, it leaves a full-length mark. Chalk and string are replaceable. Suspended from a nail, the case becomes a plumb bob for checking verticals.

Slip-Joint Pliers This all-around gripping and bending tool should be your first choice in pliers. The slotted pivot joint allows the jaws to be opened extra wide when needed. An 8″ pair is best for general work.

String Level You will find many uses for this small, lightweight level that hooks over a string. Levelling the ceiling line is one example. Buy the lightest one you can find.

Tape Measure You couldn't get started on your basement without this, and you'll use it constantly. Get one 12′ long and at least $\frac{5}{8}$″ wide — steel, of course — with a sturdy case and a locking return spring that works smoothly.

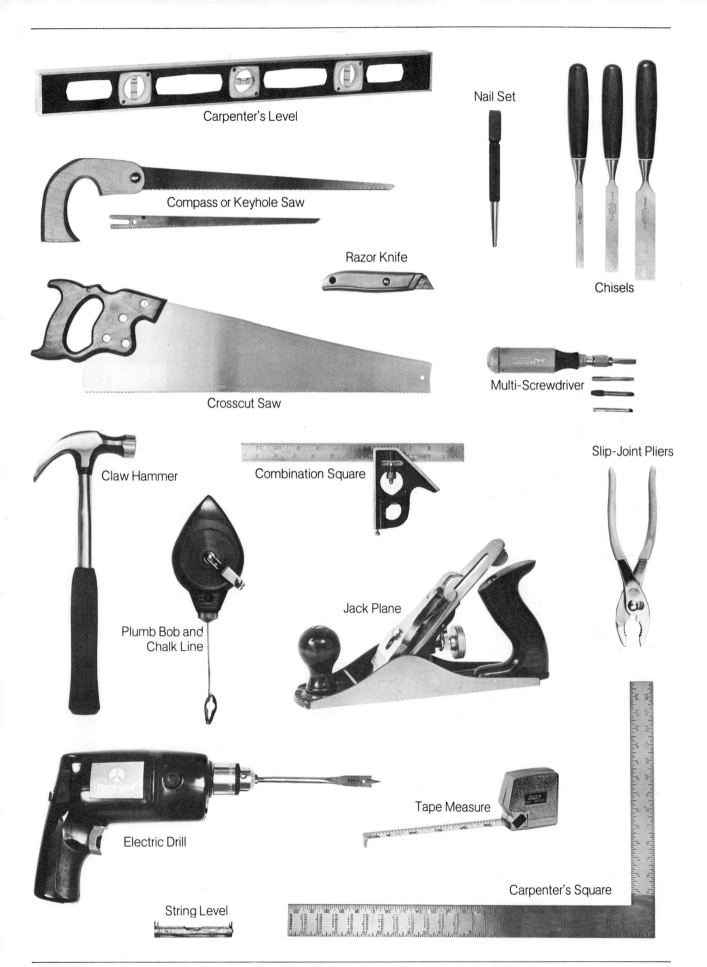

Carpenter's Level

Nail Set

Chisels

Compass or Keyhole Saw

Razor Knife

Crosscut Saw

Multi-Screwdriver

Claw Hammer

Combination Square

Slip-Joint Pliers

Jack Plane

Plumb Bob and
Chalk Line

Electric Drill

Tape Measure

Carpenter's Square

String Level

6 Concrete Fasteners

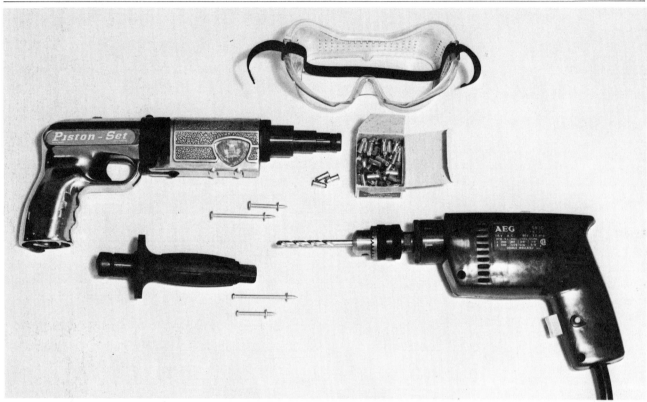

Various tools are available for driving fasteners into concrete. Top, left, is a low-velocity, piston-type, powder-actuated tool by Ramset, shown with cartridges and special nails. Below this is a Star Strikr, used with special nails and an ordinary hammer. On the right is a 2-speed hammer drill by AEG, fitted with a carbide-tipped bit.

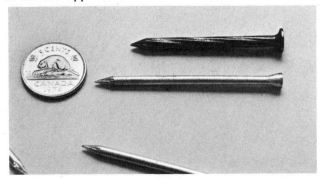

Shown here are two types of concrete or masonry nails: the spiral Ardox nail, and the less common Ucan straight nail.

There are a number of ways that strapping and framing lumber can be fastened to concrete. One of the simplest is with mastic adhesives. These are available in cartridges to fit the standard caulking gun, and are easy to apply. The concrete surface should be clean and unpainted.

Adhesives are quite satisfactory for holding short lengths of 1x2 or 1x3 strapping to a concrete wall, or for anchoring 2x4 plates to the concrete floor. However, they are not strong enough to support the weight of heavier lumber, such as 2x2 or 2x3 strapping, on to the wall. In such cases,you will have to use nails or other mechanical fasteners.

There are two kinds of concrete nails, but only one of them is widely available to the handyman. This is the thick, dark brown, spiral concrete nail sold at most hardware and building supply stores. They can be driven about ½″ into concrete with a regular hammer, but a 2-pound hammer works better. Work the nail slowly into the concrete; don't try to bash it in with brute strength. Be sure to wear protective goggles.

Much easier to drive, but harder to find, is a thin, silver-colored concrete nail that looks much like an ordinary nail but is made of very hard steel. If your hardware store doesn't have these, try a construction equipment supplier. (See photograph, lower left.)

There is also a hand-held device that allows you to drive special ringed nails into concrete without bending them. (See photograph, upper left.)

There are several different kinds of concrete anchor devices that can be used to fasten framing lumber to walls or floor. These all require a hole to be drilled in the concrete first. To do this you need a carbide-tipped bit and an electric drill. The bits are rather expensive and don't stay sharp for more than a few holes if you are using a conventional electric drill. The best tool to use is a percussion or hammer drill. This looks very much like an ordinary electric drill but it also has a 2-speed hammer action that drives the bit through even the hardest concrete very quickly.

The size of the hole depends on the size of the anchor plug you are using, but $\frac{1}{4}''$ and $\frac{5}{16}''$ are most common for this kind of work. A number of lead, aluminum, plastic, and fibre anchor plugs are available for screw, bolt and nail fasteners. The use of one kind is shown in the accompanying photographs.

Using A Nail Gun

The fastest and easiest way to drive nails into concrete, however, is with a gun-type device that uses blank cartridges and special nails. A low-velocity, piston-actuated type should be used for this work. It is perfectly safe, easy to use, and makes no more noise than a hammer. This type of unit can be rented from any tool rental shop.

A half-twist of the handle opens the breech of the nail-firing tool.

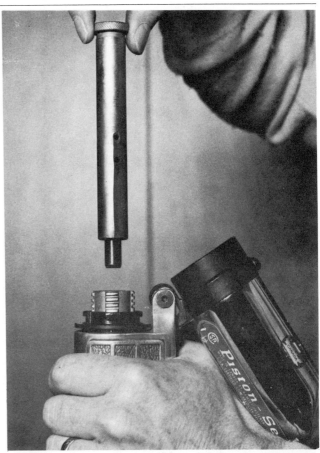

The piston is removed for loading. Because it is the piston that drives the nail, not the power charge directly, this type of unit is both safer and quieter than the high-velocity type often used in industrial work.

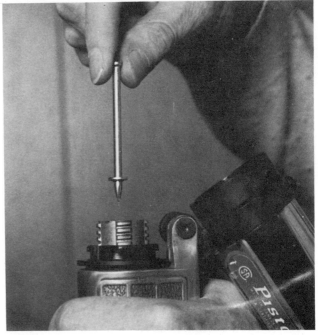

The special nail, with a slip-fit washer near the point, is dropped into the chamber. The length of the nail should allow for a penetration of about $\frac{3}{4}''$ or $1''$ into the concrete. (Nails can even be driven into steel beams, if necessary.)

Concrete Fasteners

The piston is replaced, then the firing cartridge is inserted in the breech. Cartridges come in four sizes but #3 or #4 are most commonly used for attaching nominal 2″ framing lumber to concrete.

Nail and self-contained washer are driven flush with 2x4 and 1″ into the concrete in one shot.

Nail Driver

The firing tool muzzle must be pressed tightly to surface in order to activate the trigger. The nail cannot be fired like a projectile. This and other safety devices on the tool meet CSA standards. The piston-type unit makes no more noise than an ordinary hammer hitting a nail. The cost for nail and cartridge is about 20¢ per shot.

This hand-operated tool, the Star Strikr, holds special nails straight and steady as they are driven into concrete. Nails have attached washers, similar to those used with nail guns.

Hammer Drill

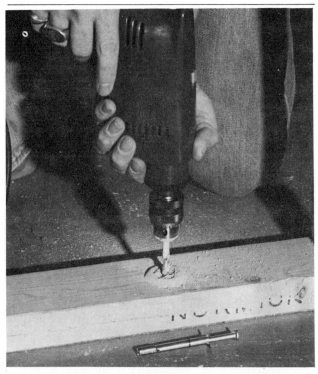

A hammer drill is the fastest way to drill holes in concrete. Switch just behind chuck converts it from a straight drill to a percussion drill that hammers as well as turns. Here a $^5/_{16}''$ hole is drilled through the 2x4 and into the concrete.

The nail section of the Dryvin is then inserted and driven home.

Special Fasteners

Several other types of concrete fasteners, including lead, plastic and fibre plugs, are shown below.

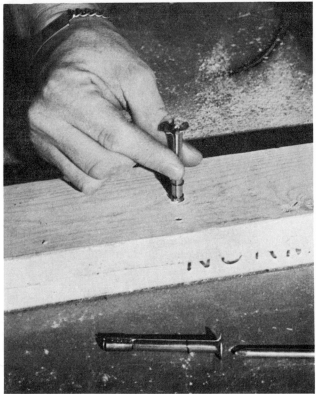

The expanding shield of a 2¾" Star Dryvin is inserted in the hole and tapped flush with the wood.

7 Strapping

It is usually necessary to strap or frame concrete basement walls with lumber in order to apply insulation and finished wall panelling. For a long time it was common practice to fasten 1x2 or 1x3 strapping or furring strips directly to the concrete walls, fill the space with insulation board, and then apply the wall panelling. This is no longer recommended for outside walls because it only allows room for ¾" of insulation, which isn't nearly enough to meet today's building requirements. Such strapping can be used, however, on concrete walls that are not exposed to the weather on the outside, such as the common wall in semi-detached houses.

On outside walls, 2x2 nailing strips must be used to allow enough space for minimum insulation. (The wall should first be painted with a bituminous dampproof coating or a waterproof paint.) At least three horizontal nailing strips should be fastened to the foundation wall, one along the top, one along the bottom, and one 4' from the bottom. Strapping spaced 24" apart will provide more nailing support for the panelling. Since the 2x2 strapping is actually only 1½" thick, 1½" foamboard with an insulation value of about R5.5 can be placed between the strapping. This meets minimum Canadian building standards but it is well below the R12 insulations value that can be achieved with 3½" batts that can be placed in a 2x4 frame wall, as described in the following section.

The 2x2 nailing strips can be fastened to the wall with concrete nails, wall anchors, or other fasteners (see Page 34). Where necessary, put wood shims or shingles behind the nailing strips to make them level.

Cut the foamboard into convenient sizes with a razor knife or a serrated bread knife, and apply the panels between the nailing strips with panel adhesive in a caulking gun cartridge, or from a can, using a spatula. (Be sure to get an adhesive that is labelled as suitable for use with polystyrene foamboard.) Apply a bead of adhesive in a continuous line about 2" in from the edge of the foamboard. Press the panels firmly in place to provide a good seal around the edges.

Electric wiring and outlets will have to be fastened to the concrete wall or the strapping first, of course, and channels must be cut in the foamboard to accommodate them. Make certain that the outlet boxes will be flush with the finished wall. Wiring can be run along the side of one of the nailing strips. To mark cutouts for the outlet boxes, just press the foamboard panels on top of them.

Plastic foamboard insulation does not require a vapor barrier, but it *must* be covered with gypsumboard or other non-inflammable material. The gypsumboard panels are fastened to the strapping with drywall nails, and the joints filled and taped to provide a smooth surface ready for papering or painting. (See Page 67).

The 2x2 strapping should be applied horizontally with concrete fasteners (see Page 34) and spaced to take the 24"-wide foamboard panels. Special foamboard adhesive is applied to the panels as shown. Adhesive also comes in caulking gun cartridges.

The 1½″ x 48″ panels of foamboard are easily cut with a razor knife to fill the spaces between the strapping. No vapor barrier is required over the foamboard.

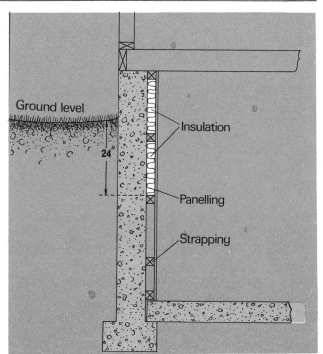

It isn't necessary to apply the foamboard insulation down to the floor; 24″ below ground level is enough. But the horizontal strapping must be continued down to the floor to provide nailing support for the gypsumboard.

Gypsumboard panelling is nailed to the strapping, then the joints are taped and filled as described on Page 67. Wood or hardboard panelling will not provide as much fire protection.

Strapping and foamboard can also be applied vertically, but care must be taken to centre a nailing strip every 48″ along the wall to accommodate the panelling. With horizontal strapping, this isn't necessary.

8 Framing

By far the best and most common way of panelling a concrete wall is to build a complete, new frame wall in front of it, using either 2x3 or 2x4 framing lumber (2x3 is cheaper, but 2x4 provides more space for insulation and is recommended for basement wall construction today). This frame wall should extend straight up from floor to ceiling, even if the foundation wall goes only part way and is framed on top.

A frame wall consists of a top plate and a bottom plate, with vertical posts or studs between them and horizontal blocking or girts between the studs. (It isn't necessary to double the top plate in basement construction, because the walls are not required to support a load.)

Where 4' x 8' panelboards such as plywood, hardboard or gypsumboard are to be applied, the studs should be spaced 16" apart on centres, with a single line of girts between the studs for additional nailing support.

If you plan to panel the wall with lumber such as barnboard or tongue-and-groove V-joint, the studs need only be spaced 4' apart, with two horizontal lines of girts between them. This stud spacing can be insulated with two rows of 23" friction-fit batts, or with several lengths of the more common 15" batts cut to fill the space. These will hold themselves in place until the polyethylene vapor barrier is applied.

Both forms of framing — 16" and 48" stud spacing — are shown in the illustrations on the opposite page.

Dampproofing

Normally the wood frame wall will not be in direct contact with the concrete foundation wall. Because of minor irregularities in the concrete surface and a slight cove at the base of the wall, there will usually be a space of a fraction of an inch between the concrete and the wood. This is desirable, because damp concrete promotes the growth of decay organisms in the wood.

In cases where the wood frame will be touching the concrete, however, the foundation wall should first be painted with an asphalt emulsion or concrete wall paint. The framing lumber can also be brushed with wood preservative.

Lumber Selection

Because the lumber used for framing will be hidden behind the panelling and is not required to support a load, a relatively inexpensive, low-grade lumber can be used. Utility and Stud grades are quite adequate. Fir, hemlock and spruce are the most common woods used for construction lumber, but use whatever is available and cheapest in your area.

Most construction lumber is simply air-dried, but more kiln-dried lumber is now being used for framing. It is drier, lighter, stronger and much less inclined to warp and twist. But whether you use air-dried or kiln-dried lumber, don't bring it inside the house until you're ready to use it. Leave it outdoors, but covered. Even kiln-dried lumber can warp if it sits around a warm, dry basement for a few weeks before it is used.

If your walls are going to be less than 7'3" high, you may be able to cut the cost of framing lumber by buying 7' studs instead of the standard 8' lengths. These shorter studs often sell for as much as 33% less than the standard length.

Use your floor plan to estimate the amount of framing lumber you will need. A standard 16" stud wall requires more lumber than the 48" stud spacing. For the former, figure on one stud length for every foot of wall ... allowing for girts, corner blocking and other framing items. For a 48" stud wall, allow one stud length for every 2' of wall.

To determine how much lumber you need for the top and bottom plates, simply multiply the perimeter of the room by 2.

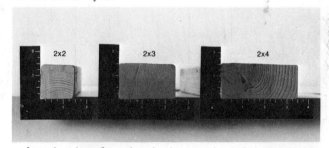

Lumber is referred to by its nominal size, not its actual size. In framing lumber, the difference is ½", so a 2x4 really only measures 1½" x 3½". Remember this when measuring wall framing.

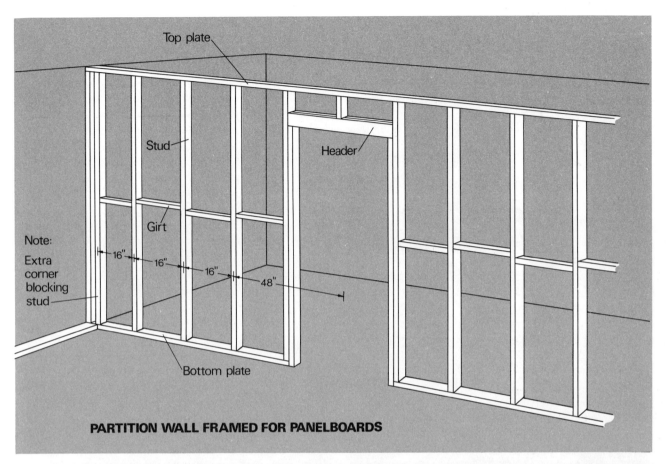

PARTITION WALL FRAMED FOR PANELBOARDS

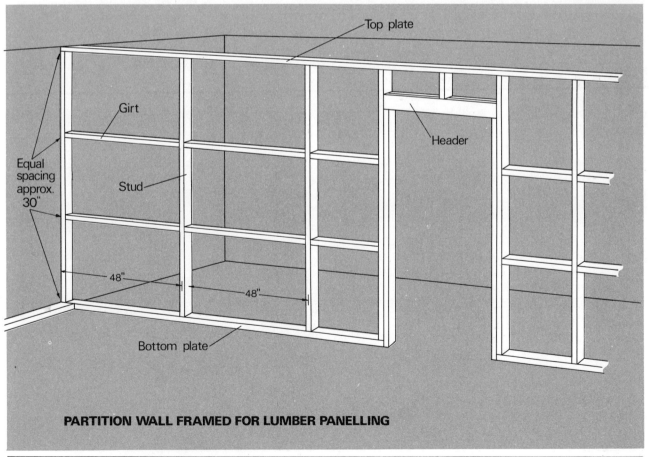

PARTITION WALL FRAMED FOR LUMBER PANELLING

33

Framing

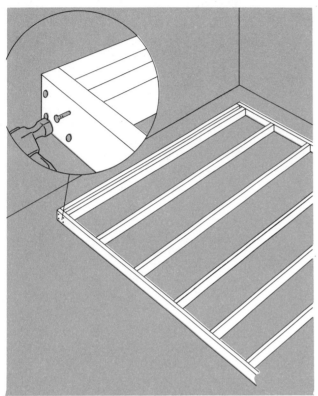

There are two schools of thought about how to put up a stud frame wall. Some experts believe that the best way is to build the wall flat on the floor and about ½″ shorter than the floor-to-joist height, then raise it into position, and wedge and nail it in place. Most carpenters, however, prefer to place the top and bottom plates first, then put in the studs one by one. There are minor advantages to both methods, though either works perfectly.

Start first on the longest outside wall and use a chalk line to mark the location of the bottom plate on the concrete floor. Measure out from the wall the width of your framing lumber (either 2½″ or 3½″) at each end of the wall. Have someone hold the end of the chalk line as you draw it out along the floor between these points. When it is in position, hold it against the floor, draw it tight, then snap it with your fingers to leave a straight, sharp chalk mark on the floor as a guide to the placement of your bottom plate.

If you find that a vent pipe or drain pipe is in the way, either move the wall out to pass it or skip the obstruction and box it in later. (See Page 46 .)

If you want to build the wall frame on the floor and raise it into position, lay out your top and bottom plates first. A 10′ section of wall is enough to lift; if the wall is longer, build it in several sections and butt the plates together.

Place the top and bottom plates together and mark the position of the studs on both of them so that they will line up properly. As you see in the illustration below, two studs are needed at the end of the wall in order to provide a nailing support for the panelling in the corner. The second stud is placed just ½″ away from the end one if you are using 2x3 framing, and 1½″ away from it if you are using 2x4 framing. Succeeding studs are spaced every 16″, centre to centre (or 16″ *on centres* as it is usually referred to). Measure and mark these positions on the top and bottom plates.

The most important studs are the ones that fall every 48″ from the corner, because this is where the panel joints will fall. It is essential to have a stud centred exactly at this point so that both panel edges can be nailed to it. If you make sure that every third stud is plumb and centred on 48″ your panelling will be much easier to put up.

Measure the distance from the floor to the lowest ceiling joist and cut all your studs 3½″ shorter than this. This will leave a ½″ space between the top of the frame wall and the lowest joist, which is necessary in order to be able to raise it into place. The space will be filled with a shingle or a wedge of scrap wood.

One advantage of building the wall on the floor is that you can nail the studs in place through the plates, as shown in the illustration, rather than having to toenail them, which you must do if you are building vertically against the concrete wall. Use 3½″ common nails.

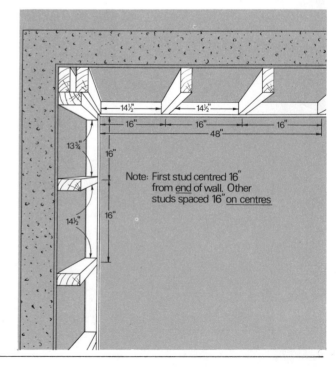

Note: First stud centred 16″ from end of wall. Other studs spaced 16″ on centres

When the wall section is assembled, raise it in place along the chalk line on the floor and wedge it against the joists. Use a carpenter's level to get the wall plumb, then nail the top plate to the joists. Fasten the bottom plate with concrete nails or other fasteners (see Page 34).

If the joists run parallel to the wall, nail short lengths of framing lumber between them every 4' and nail the top plate to these as shown in the photograph above.

When the wall is in place, nail the girts (14½″ long) between the studs for additional panelling support. They are easier to nail if they are staggered as shown below. Stagger the girts 48″ up or down to allow the plates to accommodate the 48″ insulation batts without cutting.

Framing in Place

If you prefer to build the frame wall in place, first fasten the bottom plate to the floor along the chalk line with panel adhesive or concrete fasteners. (If you use panel adhesive, you'll have to let it harden for 24 hours before building the wall.)

Use a plumb bob to locate and mark the position of the top plate on the ceiling joists directly over the bottom plate, as shown in the illustration below. Nail the top plate along this line. (As shown in the photograph on the left, if the ceiling joists are not at right-angles to the wall you will have to nail short lengths of framing lumber between them and nail the top plate to these.)

Measure and cut each stud separately and toenail it to the top and bottom plates. Be sure to locate the end studs as shown and check them with a carpenter's level to make sure they are plumb.

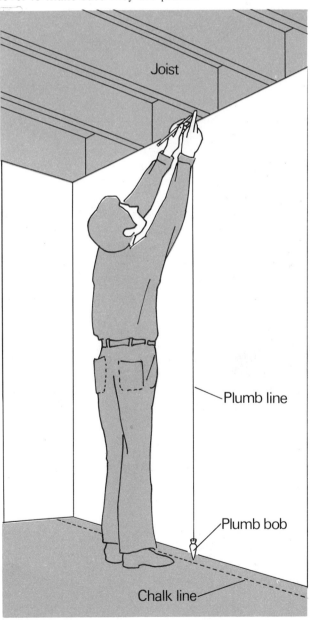

Joist

Plumb line

Plumb bob

Chalk line

Framing

An easy way to space studs 16″ on centres is to cut a piece of framing lumber 14½″ long and use this as a spacer between studs and as a support for toenailing. If the first stud is perfectly straight, it won't be necessary to check all the others with a level.

To provide firmer support for the wall panelling, nail girts between the studs about halfway up the wall, staggering them as shown in the previous photograph.

If you are building a frame wall that is to be panelled with barnboard or other lumber, space the studs on 48″ centres with two lines of girts, as shown in the illustration on Page 41.

Floating Walls

In some areas of Canada, mainly the Prairies, the clay soil expands and contracts under the basement floor due to seasonal moisture changes. This often causes cracks and floor movement, making it inadvisable to build a basement stud wall tight under the ceiling joists. Build a "floating wall" instead, by leaving about 1½″ space between the top plate and the lowest joist or other ceiling member. Drill ¼″ holes in the top plate where it is to be fastened to the joists, then drive in 6″ spikes, leaving about 1½″ of the spikes below the plate, as shown below. This allows the wall to move up and down, but still holds it firmly in position.

A suspended ceiling (see Page 78) works best with this type of wall construction.

Framing Windows and Doors

Rough-frame around windows as shown in the photograph opposite. Finishing details will be given later. If the window is large, it may be easier to frame a separate wall section to fit underneath it rather than try to build it into the wall frame.

If possible, doorways should be centred where two wall panels will join. Half the doorway will be cut into the side of each panel. This makes a neater wall pattern than having a small strip of panelling on one side of the door, but it isn't always possible to arrange.

Rough-framing for a door is shown in the illustration, opposite. The two outside studs should be spaced 4¾″ farther apart than the width of the door. For the common 30″ door the two outside studs would be 34¾″ apart. Check with a carpenter's level to make sure they are perfectly plumb, then cut out the bottom plate between them.

Next measure the height of your door, add 1½″, and cut two pieces of framing lumber this length. Nail these to the cut end of the bottom plate and to the outside studs, as shown. Now cut two pieces of framing lumber to fit across the top of these studs, forming the header. These are usually placed vertically, as shown in the detail drawing. A short, "cripple" stud is then cut and nailed between the header and the top plate.

(A doorway can be rough-framed with a single stud on either side and a single header, but double-framing gives a much firmer and more solid door.)

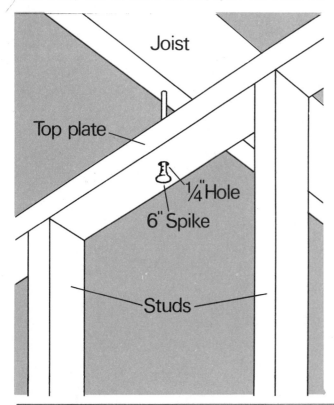

Joist

Top plate

¼″ Hole

6″ Spike

Studs

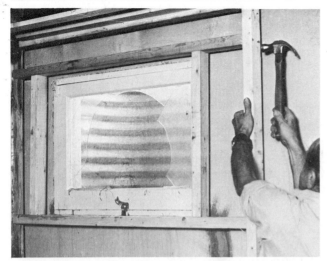
Existing windows are simply rough-framed as shown here, being sure to leave enough room for the finish framing and hardware.

Deep-set windows can be rough-framed to the concrete, then faced with panelling. Trim will be added next.

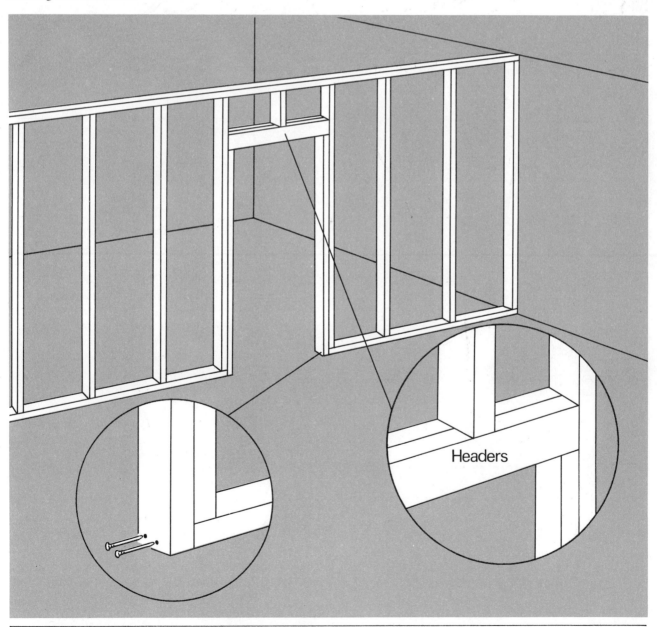

Headers

Framing

Partition Walls

Interior partition walls are framed the same way as the outside walls. They should be drawn on the floor first, so that the location can be checked and moved if necessary. To make sure the walls are at right angles, use the 3-4-5 rule, as shown in the illustration.

To mark a right-angle at point A, measure 3' along the existing wall to point B. With a felt marker tied to a 4' length of string held at point A, draw an arc on the floor through C. With the felt marker attached to a 5' length of cord held at point B, draw another arc to intersect the first one at C. A line drawn from A through C will be at right angles to the wall AB. A chalk line laid from A through C and across the floor will mark the correct position for the partition wall.

The correct way to join two stud walls at right angles is shown in the illustration below.

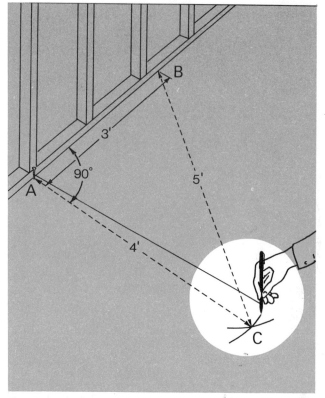

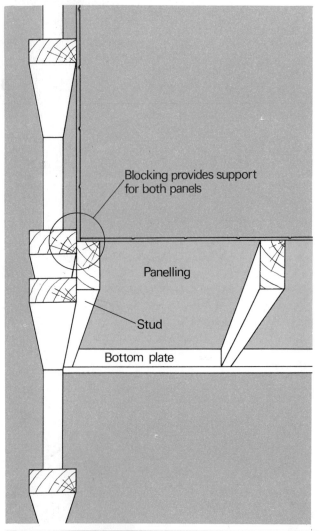

Blocking provides support for both panels

Panelling

Stud

Bottom plate

Boxing In

There never was a basement ceiling that didn't have a beam, drain pipe, heating plenum, or other projection that needed to be hidden when the basement was finished. If there is more than 7'3" headroom under the lowest ceiling projection, the best thing to do is put in a suspended ceiling under everything (see Page 78).

But often there isn't enough room for this, and you must apply the ceiling tiles to the joists to have the headroom you need. In this case you'll have to box in the projections.

Don't try to build a box around everything, however, or you'll end up with a lot of ugly bumps on the ceiling, and the extra headroom between them won't be of much use. It will look much better if you drop part of the ceiling to cover a number of projections, taking the lower ceiling right over to a wall.

It may be possible, for instance, to enclose a warm-air plenum inside a dropped ceiling over the bar, with built-in pot lights to shine down on the counter.

If a plenum or beam is within 3' or 4' of the wall and parallel to it, it will look better if you drop the ceiling from the plenum over to the wall.

But if the room isn't being finished fancy, you may

not have to box in the plenum at all. It has a neat box-like shape, and if you paint it flat white with latex paint it will blend with the ceiling and be almost unnoticeable (see photograph, bottom right). This also saves a couple of inches headroom.

Ladders

Boxing in isn't as difficult as it looks. All you do is build "ladders" with 2x2 or 1x2 lumber, the "rungs" spaced about 16″ apart. Nail one ladder to the ceiling joists on each side of the projection, and connect the ladders across the bottom with nailing strips, as illustrated. An alternative method of building the ladders is shown below.

In some cases it may be easier to use scrap pieces of low-grade lumber or plywood for the side of the box, as shown in the photographs.

It is usually best to cover the boxing with inexpensive, ½″ sheathing grade plywood, (photograph top,

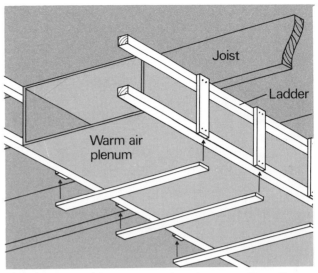

right), to provide a solid surface for the ceiling tiles or decorative plywood.

The same procedure is used to box in vertical projections such as vent stacks and drains.

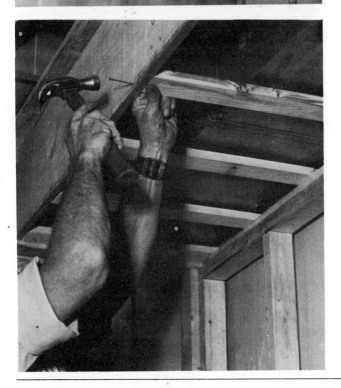

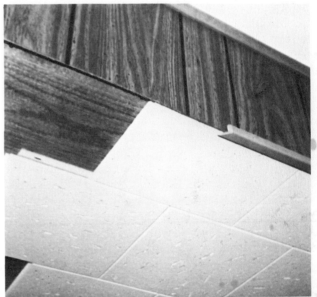

9 Steel Framing

Although very few home handymen realize it yet, steel studs are a lot faster, easier, and more convenient to use than conventional wood framing. Here are some of the advantages:

● Steel studs are much lighter than wood. You can carry all the steel framing members needed to build a basement recreation room under one arm. They also take up much less space.

● Steel framing never warps or twists out of shape, no matter how long they lay around before you use them.

● You can put up a steel frame wall in less than a quarter of the time it would take to build it out of lumber. Once the top and bottom tracks are fastened, the studs are merely snapped in place.

The only disadvantage is that you can't nail anything to steel studs — adhesives or special screw-nails must be used. (Steel-stud walls cannot be used to support a load, either, but this is no disadvantage in basement building because none of the frame walls are load-bearing.)

As far as cost is concerned, steel and wood are about the same. But steel framing is not as easy to find. Few buildings supply stores carry it yet, but it is widely used in commercial drywall construction, so any distributor of drywall panelling should be able to tell you where steel stud framing is available in your city. Or look in the Yellow Pages under *Drywall Contractors' Equipment and Supplies.*

Galvanized steel framing comes in 8' lengths and in widths that correspond to standard framing lumber. The 3⅝" stud size (equivalent to a 2x4) is recommended for outside walls that must be insulated. Interior partition walls can be 2½" studs (equivalent to a 2x3) but it complicates matters to change sizes and the saving is small. It's better to use 3⅝" studs throughout. The top and bottom track are not the same shape as the studs, but come in the same sizes. The studs are C-shaped, with stiffening ribs and knurled edges to bite screws. The track is perfectly flat on the bottom and the sides are angled in to provide a spring grip to hold the studs in place.

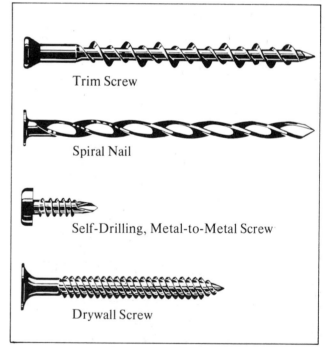

Trim Screw

Spiral Nail

Self-Drilling, Metal-to-Metal Screw

Drywall Screw

Ordinary nails can't be used with steel framing, but a number of fasteners are available, some of them developed specially for applying gypsumboard panelling to steel studs. Special self-drilling and self-tapping sheet metal screws have also been produced for fastening metal to metal. Both of these should be driven with a power screwdriver, available at any tool rental store. Spiral nails and trim screws are used to fasten steel framing to wood.

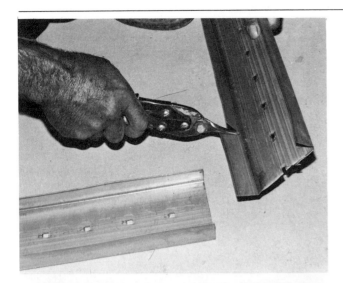

The ceiling track is fastened to the joists with ¾″ screws. (A power screwdriver is being used here.) Where the track is running parallel to the joists, attach 2x4 nailing girts between the joists every 2′ or so.

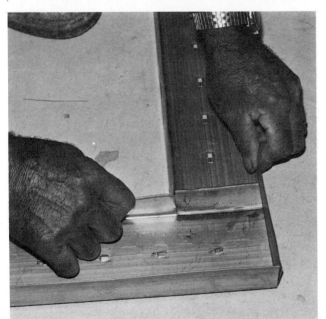

Before you install either the ceiling track or the floor track (corresponding to the top plate and bottom plate in wood framing) cut the overlapping corner joints as shown in the photographs above.

Use a stud and carpenter's level to find the location for the bottom track. Do this at each end of the wall, then snap a chalk line along the floor between the marks to show the position of the bottom track. (In some cases it may be better to fasten the bottom track first and use a plumb bob or carpenter's level to locate the top track.)

Steel Framing

The bottom track can be attached with concrete nails, but panel adhesive is easier and faster. Run a bead of adhesive down the centre of the track location, then press the track in place and allow the adhesive to set for a couple of hours or more before putting in the studs.

Studs are cut about ¼″ shorter than the actual distance between the top and bottom tracks, then simply twisted into position. The spring edge of the track grips the knurled edge of the studs well enough to hold

them in position, but they can be moved easily if adjustment is required. If you want to hold a stud in place permanently, use a ³⁄₈″ self-tapping metal screw, starting the hole with a nail or centrepunch. A crimping tool can also be used (see illustration opposite).

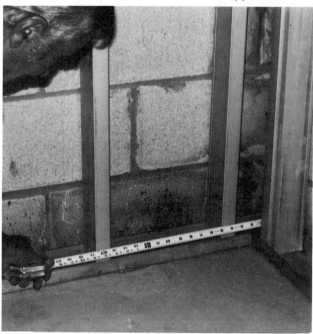

Corner studs for drywall panelling are located 2″ out from the corner to allow room for the screw gun. Remaining studs are spaced 16″ on centres as usual.

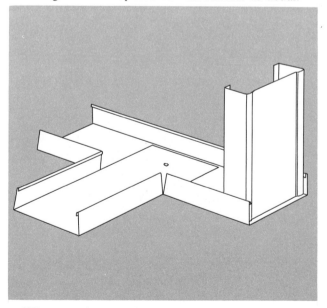

Where an intersecting wall is required, the ceiling and floor tracks are simply cut and overlapped as shown above. Studs should be placed close to the corner to support the edge of the panelboard.

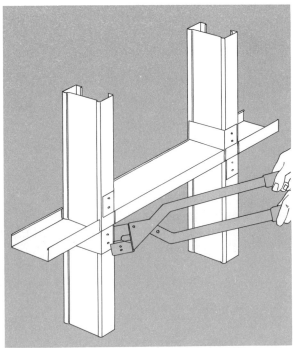

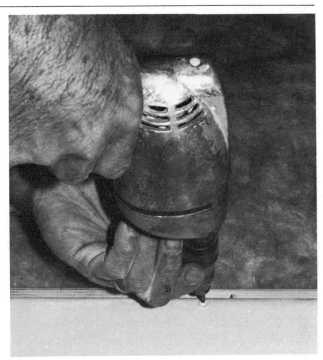

Girts are not usually needed in a steel-stud wall, but if required they can be made very easily from sections of track 6″ longer than the stud spacing. Cut the flanges at both ends and bend to form a right angle. Fasten with self-tapping screws or a crimping tool. The next girt is put in the other way up, as shown above.

Gypsumboard panelling is applied over the vapor barrier with special drywall screws. On interior walls that are not insulated and require no vapor barrier, any type of panelling can be applied to the steel studs with panel adhesive (see Page 65).

Friction-fit batts, 3½″ thick, are pressed in place between the studs. The corner gap must be filled, too. Polyethylene vapor barrier is then applied over the entire wall and temporarily held in place with masking tape.

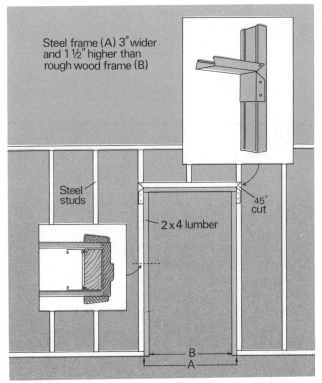

Steel frame (A) 3″ wider and 1½″ higher than rough wood frame (B)

Steel studs

2 x 4 lumber

45° cut

B
A

Door frames in a steel-stud wall should be made 3″ wider and 1½″ higher than the *rough* opening required. Two-by-fours are then screwed to the metal frame as shown above, using two ¾″ screws at least every 24″ and not more than 6″ from the floor or header. The finished, wood door casing and frame are then installed as described on Page 82.

10 Wiring

Doing your own electrical wiring is obviously more hazardous than putting up a stud wall or laying a tile floor, but if you are careful to take a few rather obvious precautions and follow some simple rules there is no reason why you can't put in all the lights, switches and outlets you need for your finished basement.

All provinces except Quebec permit home-owners to do their own wiring, provided a permit is obtained and the wiring is inspected before it is covered. Your local building department or hydro office can advise you of the proper procedure to follow. You are required to fill out an application form giving a rough description of the work to be done and the number of outlets to be put in. A fee of about $10 is charged and you are then given a permit to proceed with the work.

When the wiring is completed, but not covered, you notify the permit department and they will send an inspector to examine the job. He either approves the work or leaves an inspection report indicating what is wrong. If any changes are necessary, you must complete them and request another inspection. There is no extra charge for inspections.

Most electrical inspectors are glad to help a home-owner do a safe wiring job. They are concerned only with protection from fire and shock hazards, not with who does the work. The wiring regulations in the Canadian Electrical Code were written to assure such safety, and must be followed very carefully even though some of the requirements may seem arbitrary or unnecessary to the layman.

There are three Canadian books on electrical wiring that would be helpful to the home handyman:

Electrical Code Simplified, by P.S. Knight, includes simple diagrams and explanations of Canadian code requirements for home wiring. Four editions are available, covering British Columbia, Alberta, Saskatchewan and Ontario ... $3.75 each at building supply stores or directly from the author and publisher at 984 Seacote Road, Richmond, B.C.

Applications of Electrical Construction, by Robert K. Clidero and Kenneth H. Sharpe is a 296-page, illustrated, hardcover Canadian textbook on residential and industrial wiring ... $14.95. General Publishing Co. Ltd.

Wiring Installation and Maintenance for Canadians, by Harold B. Kirchner. Clearly written and illustrated ... 175 pages, $10.95. Published by McGraw-Hill Ryerson.

Two U.S. books that have been modified to meet the Canadian electrical code are *Basic Wiring* and *Advanced Wiring* in the Time-Life series on Home Repair and Improvement. Superbly illustrated and clearly written ... 128 pages, $10 softcover, $12 hardcover.

Basic Wiring

For basement lighting and convenience outlets you are only concerned with 120-volt wiring circuits. These are the circuits that are controlled by each of the 15-amp fuses or circuit breakers in your service panel. Larger fuses are only used in 240-volt circuits serving stoves, driers, air conditioners, etc., or in special fuse panels inside the stove.

Such 120-volt circuits are generally carried by a plastic-sheathed "2-wire" cable that actually contains three wires; one covered with black insulation, one covered with white insulation, and a bare ground wire. This type of cable is known as NMD 7. Fourteen gauge copper wire is most commonly used, and the full identification is 14/2 Copper NMD 7. Three-wire cable, required for some wiring situations, would be marked 14/3.

There is a very important difference between the use of the black and white wires, and it is essential that you understand this before undertaking any wiring.

Power is supplied to your house through a 3-wire cable. One of the wires is grounded, or "neutral", at zero voltage. Between the other two wires there is a potential of 240 volts, but *between each of them and the neutral wire* there is just half of this, 120 volts.

At the service panel inside your house the two "hot" wires are black and the neutral wire is white. Circuits requiring 240 volts are taken from the two black wires. All household lighting circuits, however, are connected between the white, neutral wire and one of the two black wires.

Because the white wire is grounded, theoretically you can touch it without getting a shock, but it doesn't always work that way, so it's not a good idea to try it. Only the black wire carries the voltage. Wiring circuits are designed to isolate the black wire and reduce the danger of shock or fire. Fuses and switches are always placed in the black line; the white wire runs continuously from the service panel to the last outlet in the circuit. Light sockets are wired so that the threaded shell is neutral and you won't get a shock when you are unscrewing a bulb, although this doesn't work when extension cords are used.

It is very important, therefore, to connect the black and white wires correctly throughout the circuit. When making connections to duplex receptacles, ceiling fixtures, switches, and other terminals, only black wires should be connected to the gold-colored terminals, only white wires to the silver terminals.

Grounding

Further protection against fire and shock hazard is provided by the bare ground wire in the cable. This is grounded at the service panel and must be connected to every outlet box and receptacle throughout the circuit.

The reason is very simple. If a loose black wire inside an electrical appliance touches the metal housing, the appliance itself would carry a 120-volt potential that could kill you if you picked it up. Most such appliances now have a 3-wire, grounded extension cord. The third wire is connected to the metal housing of the appliance at one end and to the ground pin in the plug at the other When it is plugged into a grounded receptacle, the current from the hot housing flows back to the service panel and blows a fuse before it can blow you.

Testing

There are many times when you will want to check for a hot wire or test a circuit to make sure it is off before touching it. This can be done with a simple neon bulb voltage tester that lights up when the probes touch a power source.

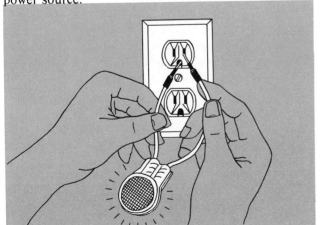

You can check the grounding of a wall receptacle, for instance, by putting one probe in the circular ground slot and the other probe into each of the prong slots in turn. The tester should light up when it is plugged into the hot slot — the slightly shorter of the two slots in

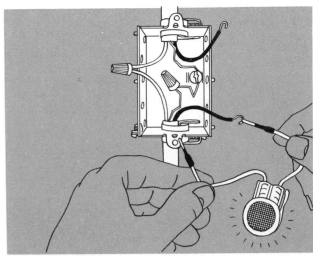

modern receptacles.

The same method is used to find out which of two or more black wires coming into an outlet box is carrying current from the service panel.

How to Proceed

All wiring connections must be made inside a metal or plastic outlet box attached to the framework of the house. Steel boxes are the most common. Duplex outlet and switch boxes are nominally 2″ wide and 3″ high and from 2″ to 3″ deep. Two or more can be ganged together by removing the side plates. The electrical code limits the number of wires permitted in each box size. A 2″ deep switch box, for instance, may only contain five #14 wires. A 3½″ deep box may have seven #14 wires. (Ground wires are not counted.)

Below, left, is a 4″ octagonal box commonly used for ceiling fixtures. At the back is a utility box used for surface-mounted switches or duplex receptacles. Centre, front, is the familiar sectional switch box. These boxes can be ganged by removing the side panels as shown on the right.

Wiring

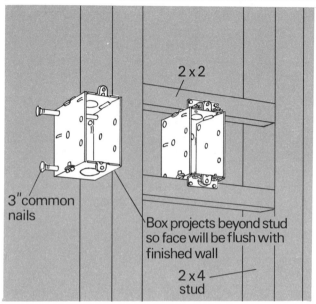

2 x 2

3" common nails

Box projects beyond stud so face will be flush with finished wall

2 x 4 stud

The first step in wiring is to fasten the appropriate boxes in the locations where they are needed. Boxes must be mounted so that their face edge will be flush with the *finished* wall. Adjustable mounting lugs are provided. Wall boxes to be placed between studs can be screwed or nailed between two horizontal, 2x2 nailing strips, as shown above, but the easiest place to fasten them is to the side of a stud, using 3" common nails through the holes provided at the back of the box.

All of the boxes have knock-out discs for cable entrance, but it is also necessary to use clamps to hold the cable in place. Some boxes have built-in clamps, but those with larger, nickel-sized knock-outs require the use of exterior clamps as shown above. It is not permissible simply to push the cable into the box through the hole; it must be clamped.

No more than ½" of cable sheathing can project into the box. At least 6" of insulated wire must be provided for connections inside the box. Use a razor knife or a special cable ripping tool to cut through the centre of the cable sheathing for 6", then fold the sheathing back and cut it off with a pair of shears. Peel and cut off the paper that is wrapped around the two wires. Use a knife or wire stripper to remove the insulation from about ⅝" of each wire, but be careful not to cut into the wire. If you do, cut it off and start again.

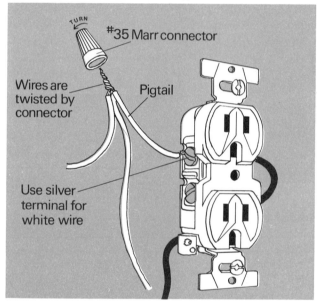

TURN

#35 Marr connector

Wires are twisted by connector

Pigtail

Use silver terminal for white wire

For screw terminal connections, bend the wire with round-nose pliers. Only one wire can be fastened to a terminal. If more than one wire must be connected to a terminal, use a pigtail or jumper wire of the same kind and color and join all the wires together with a screw-on or Marr connector. Use a #31 connector for two #14 wires, a #35 connector for up to four #14 wires. Push the straight wires into the connector and twist it clockwise. No bare wire should be exposed.

Adding New Wiring

The first thing to do when you want to add new wiring in a house is look for an existing wiring circuit that can carry the additional outlets. Then you can simply tap into this line, as we will show. If you can't find such a circuit, you will have to go back to the service panel and find an open circuit position.

As we have seen, every 120-volt household wiring circuit is controlled by a 15-amp fuse or circuit breaker in the main service panel. What you need to do now is find out exactly what lights or outlets are on each circuit, and mark this on a wiring table like the one shown here. (Such a table will also come in handy in locating blown fuses quickly and finding the safest location for plugging in heavy current appliances such as hair driers and portable heaters.)

The procedure is simple but tedious. First make a list of all the lights and outlets in the house. Then number the fuses or circuit breakers in the main service panel and draw vertical columns on your wiring table for each of them, as shown in our sample.

Open circuit #1 by removing the fuse or throwing the breaker switch, then take your wiring table and a light on a short extension cord and proceed through the house, testing every light and outlet. Check *both* outlets in each duplex receptacle; you will find some that are connected to two separate circuits. Watch, too, for the ones that are controlled by a wall switch. And don't overlook outdoor outlets and lights.

If the light or outlet is still working, place a check mark on your table in the circuit column you are testing. Where the power is off, mark an X.

Return to the service panel, replace the fuse in the circuit just tested and open the next one. Then proceed through the house again, testing every light and outlet. This will get faster as you learn where each outlet or switch is located, and as more of them are checked off.

When you have finished the last circuit check you should have one X against every light and outlet in the house, and perhaps two against counter-height outlets in the kitchen and laundry room. Looking down the columns you will notice that some circuits have only one or two outlets on them. Such "appliance outlets" are required in the kitchen and laundry room. The furnace also requires a separate outlet. Other circuits, however, are allowed to have as many as 12 light or duplex receptacle outlets, so if you find one with, say, less than 6 outlets or switch-controlled lights, you can probably use this to supply up to 6 additional lights or outlets in the basement.

The maximum amount of current that can be carried at one time by a single 15-amp circuit is 1,440 watts, so total up the wattage in the lights or appliances that are presently using the circuit to make sure there is enough current available to serve your basement needs.

Tapping into an Existing Circuit

There are several possible places where you can tap into an under-used circuit. One or more can be used, as convenient. Be sure to disconnect the circuit at the service panel, however, before touching it. Use a voltage tester (Page 53) to be certain that the power is off.

New wiring can be run from a duplex receptacle provided it is not controlled by a switch. The easiest to use is an end-of-the-run receptacle, which is easy to identify because it only has one cable entering the box.

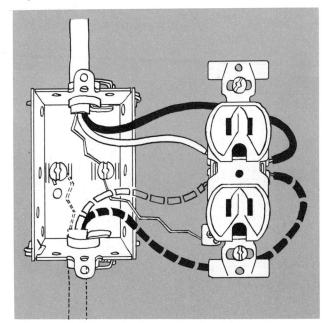

Even if it is in the base of an upstairs wall, you can probably drill up through the floor into the wall and fish a new cable up from the basement to the outlet box. The black and white wires from the new cable are simply attached to the spare gold and silver terminals on the duplex receptacle, as shown above. The new ground wire can be connected to the box with a screw.

HOUSEHOLD CIRCUIT CHART

	FUSE 1	2	3	4	5	6	7	8
	✓	✓	✓	X	✓	✓	✓	✓
Driveway light	✓	✓	✓	X	✓	✓	✓	✓
Porch light	✓	✓	✓	X	✓	✓	✓	✓
Garage light	✓	✓	✓	X	✓	✓	✓	✓
Garage outlet	✓	X	✓	✓	✓	✓	✓	✓
Patio outlet		X	✓	✓	✓	✓	✓	✓
Entrance light	✓	X	✓	✓	✓	✓	✓	✓
Living room S wall outlet	✓	X	✓	✓	✓	✓	✓	✓
W wall "	✓	X	✓	✓	✓	✓	✓	✓
E wall "	✓	X	✓	✓	✓	✓	✓	✓
Dining room ceiling light	✓	✓	X	✓	✓	✓	✓	✓
W wall outlet	✓	X	✓	✓	✓	✓	✓	✓
Kitchen ceiling light	✓	✓	X	✓	✓	✓	✓	✓
counter outlet	✓	✓	✓	X	✓	✓	✓	✓
fridge outlet	✓	✓	✓	✓	✓	X	✓	✓
dishwasher	✓	✓	✓	✓	X	✓	✓	✓
Back hall light	✓	X	✓	✓	✓	✓	✓	✓
Master bedroom ceiling	✓	X	✓	✓	✓	✓	✓	✓
S wall outlet	✓	X	✓	✓	✓	✓	✓	✓
E wall outlet	✓	X	✓	✓	✓	✓	✓	✓
BR 2 ceiling light	✓	✓	X	✓	✓	✓	✓	✓
desk light	✓	✓	X	✓	✓	✓	✓	✓
W wall outlet	✓	✓	X	✓	✓	✓	✓	✓
BR 3 ceiling light	✓	✓	X	✓	✓	✓	✓	✓
bed light	✓	✓	X	✓	✓	✓	✓	✓
S wall outlet	✓	✓	X	✓	✓	✓	✓	✓
Bathroom ceiling light	✓	✓	✓	X	✓	✓	✓	✓
sink light	✓	✓	✓	X	✓	✓	✓	✓
razor outlet	✓	✓	✓	X	✓	✓	✓	✓
Basement stair light	✓	✓						
Furnace room light	✓							
Furnace								
Workshop ceiling								

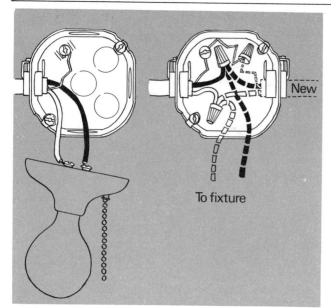

To fixture

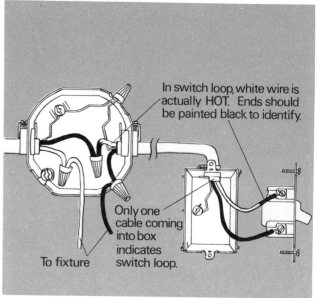

In switch loop, white wire is actually HOT. Ends should be painted black to identify.

Only one cable coming into box indicates switch loop.

To fixture

Many basements have porcelain ceiling light fixtures controlled by pull-chains (above, left). It is easy to add new wiring to these. Unscrew the porcelain fixture and pull it down from the ceiling. If there is only one cable coming into the box, as shown on the left, then you will be able to connect a second cable by using black and white jumper wires and making new connections as shown by the dotted lines in the illustration right.

There is a third possibility. If the ceiling fixture is controlled by a wall switch that has only one cable coming into it, the wires in the ceiling box may look like this, with a white wire apparently connected to a black wire. As you can see, however, one cable is simply a "switch loop" and is acting like a black, hot wire carrying current to and from the switch. The white wire in this cable is supposed to be identified as a hot wire with a dab of black paint or a short piece of black tape at each terminal but electricians often overlook this.

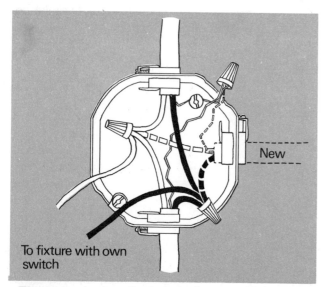

New

To fixture with own switch

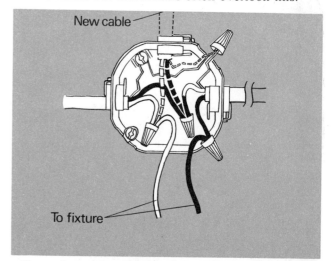

New cable

To fixture

The example described above is an end-of-the-run light fixture. If it is a middle-of-the-run fixture it will have two cables coming into the box and the black and white fixture wires will be connected to the matching wires in both cables, as shown in the illustration above. You can see here how a new cable can be connected to these.

To tap into this ceiling box you must first determine which is the supply cable and which is the switch loop cable. If it is correctly wired, the white fixture wire will be connected to the supply cable and the black fixture wire to the switch loop. Use a voltage tester to check, however, as described on Page 53 Connections for the new cable are indicated by the dotted lines.

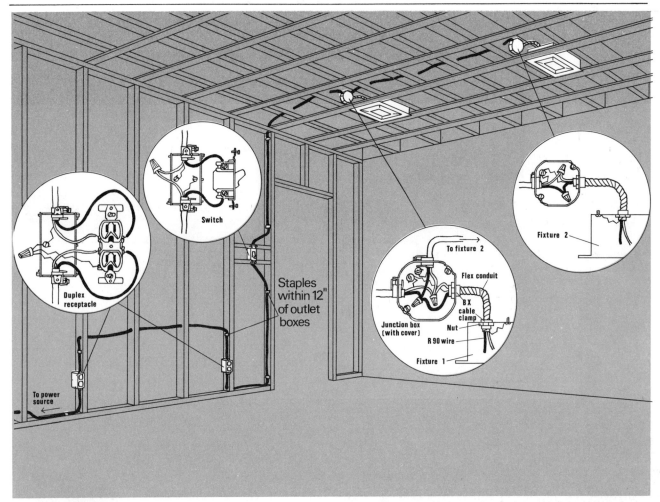

Staples within 12" of outlet boxes

To power source

Duplex receptacle

Switch

To fixture 2

Flex conduit

B X cable clamp

Junction box (with cover)

Nut

R 90 wire

Fixture 1

Fixture 2

Ceiling Fixtures

Because ceiling height is often limited in a basement, recessed lighting fixtures are the type most commonly used. These can be either flourescent (tubes) or incandescent (bulbs). Due to the relatively high temperatures that can occur inside recessed incandescent fixtures, they must be wired with special, high-temperature wire, insulated with asbestos or other fireproof material. R90 wire is the minimum requirement (this number refers to the maximum temperature in degrees Celsius).

Some recessed fixtures have built-in junction boxes where the regular house wiring cable can be connected to the special fixture wire, but these are not usually found on the inexpensive recessed fixtures available to the home-owner. A separate junction box will therefore be required for each fixture, and these should be connected as shown in the above illustration.

Note that a length of flexible metal conduit must be used to protect the special wire running from the fixture to the junction box. About 18" of this wire is usually provided with the fixture. The flexible conduit is available from electrical supply stores or from building supply dealers who carry these recessed ceiling fix-

tures. You will also need special clamps to fasten the flexible conduit to the junction box and the fixture.

In the example shown here, two ceiling lights are controlled by the one wall switch. If there was only one fixture, it would be connected like fixture #2 here. If more ceiling fixtures are to be controlled by the same switch — two more lights at the other end of the room, for instance — then #2 fixture would be wired the same as #1, and the NMD 7 cable would continue to fixture #3 (wired as #1) and then to fixture #4, which would be wired as #2 is shown here.

The above illustration shows a typical basement wiring circuit, incorporating duplex wall receptacles and switch-controlled light fixtures. Additional receptacles could be provided according to the capacity of the circuit (see Page 55). Other switches and lights can be tapped from these receptacles if 3½" deep boxes are used to accommodate the extra wires.

Fluorescent ceiling fixtures are wired in essentially the same way, the only difference being that there is no need for the use of high-temperature wire inside the fixture. It is not necessary, therefore, to have separate junction boxes for each fixture; the connections to the regular wiring cable can be made inside the metal housing of the fixture itself. Be sure to attach the ground wire as well; this is essential for the operation of some fluorescent fixtures.

11 Panelling

Which Comes First . . . Walls or Ceiling?

If you are going to use ceiling tiles, the strapping should be applied before the walls are panelled (see Page 76). Don't put up the tiles, however, until the walls are done, otherwise they may be damaged when you are installing the panels. But if you plan to put up a suspended ceiling (see Page 78), don't start until the walls have been panelled.

Doing the rough framing is the hardest and slowest part of building a basement room, but if it's been done right, the next step, panelling, will be very easy. And very satisfying, too, because the room quickly begins to take shape around you just the way you imagined it.

There's a vast selection of panelling materials to choose from, at prices running from as little as 15¢ a square foot for the softboards to as much as $1 a square foot for some of the prefinished hardwood veneers.

Most panelling materials come in 4′ x 8′ sheets, $3/16''$ to $1/4''$ thick, but various kinds of nominal 1″ panelling lumber are also available. The 4′ x 8′ panels are easiest to apply, and also cheaper. And, since most of them are prefinished, there's nothing more to do after they are put up.

Your choice of panelling depends on your budget and your taste, but the style of the room and the amount of use it will be given should also influence your selection. A children's playroom, for instance, might best be panelled with a durable, vinyl-covered gypsumboard that can take a lot of abuse. On the other hand, if you want to build an impressive library/den, you might want to panel it with an exotic hardwood.

For general appearance and ease of maintenance, a textured wall surface is usually considered better than a smooth one. Wood panelling looks better with a natural grain texture rather than a glossy finish. Also, a panel grooved to look like random-width planks will show marks less easily than one with a smooth surface.

You'll find that all but the cheapest, simulated-wood panelboards are now produced with an embossed woodgrain texture. Textures can also be achieved with coarse fabric wallcoverings, plaster-based paints, wood shingles, barnboard and even thin slices of brick.

Softboard

The cheapest finished panelling material is softboard. This is very similar to the material used in the well-known ceiling tiles. Just a shade under $1/2''$ thick, the 4′ x 8′ panels are available with a factory-applied, white primer coat that can be used either as a final finish or over-painted.

The material is very soft and must be handled carefully to avoid damage. The corners are easily broken and the surface can be scratched with a fingernail. It is best applied with $1\frac{1}{4}''$ ringed, flat-headed flooring nails (the nailheads can be touched up with a spot of paint).

Softboard absorbs sound better than other panelling materials (see Page 91) and has more insulation value too, but not enough to be of much significance.

Hardboard

Made of compressed wood fibres, hardboard is familiar to most of us as a brown, smooth-faced panelboard, $1/8''$ to $1/4''$ thick, with a rough, wire screen pattern on the back. Although it can be painted or papered (a primer-sealer is recommended, except for latex paints), this standard hardboard is rarely used for wall panelling. The decorative hardboards, however, offer a wide range of prefinished surfaces in colored fabric textures, imitation brick, stone, stucco, tile and printed woodgrain reproductions that are realistic enough to fool anyone but an expert, as can be seen in the simulated stone pattern shown in the following photograph.

Hardwood Plywood

Although most people think of this group in terms of the exotic furniture veneers like pecan, rosewood and walnut, it also includes one of the softest and cheapest woods around...Philippine "mahogany", actually lauan. (True furniture mahogany comes from India, Africa or Central America.)

Most lauan plywood is rotary cut, the veneer is peeled off the log like unrolling a paper towel. This process is fast and efficient, but the grain pattern of the veneer is not very interesting. Ribbon-cut or flat-cut veneer, on the other hand, is sliced off a square block of wood, producing a much more attractive grain pattern. A limited amount of ribbon-cut lauan "mahogany" is available, at about twice the price of the rotary cut panels but still a lot cheaper than the other hardwood veneers.

The best finish for lauan is a satin urethane varnish. Oil finishes or penetrating sealers do not give enough protection to the soft wood. The porous, open grain of the surface should be filled before it is varnished. Brush a thin paste filler on with the grain, let it set for about 20 minutes, then wipe it off across the grain with a coarse cloth. Allow the filler to dry for 24 hours, then sand lightly, dust and varnish.

Inexpensive lauan plywood is also used to produce a variety of real wood panels printed or overlaid with a simulated-woodgrain finish. These are similar to the hardboard woodgrain panels already discussed, but they are less subject to swelling or distortion due to humidity changes. They are not, however, true hardwood veneer panels; they are printed imitations, though very good ones.

These decorative hardboards constitute the great majority of panelling materials sold for basement remodelling. They are available in virtually all of the popular woodgrains, including oak, walnut, pecan, teak, cedar, hickory, ash, pine, rosewood and African mahogany. The simulated-woodgrain surface is a printed paper overlay protected with a tough plastic finish, and is usually grooved to represent random-width V-joint, plank panelling. The better panels are even embossed with a remarkably realistic woodgrain texture. Cheaper ones have a smooth surface.

Hardboard has one weakness; it tends to swell and buckle if it gets damp, a condition that is not uncommon in basements. For this reason it must be allowed to adjust to the humidity of the room for two or three days before being used. (See Page 63.)

Panelling

The finest panelboards are the prefinished, exotic hardwood veneers. Most expensive are the rare woods in book-matched veneers and sequence-matched panels. Book-matched means the veneer slices are folded open in pairs so that the grain pattern in one is a mirror reflection of the other. Sequence-matched panels are numbered to follow the progression of the grain slices off the log.

Panels like this can cost $1.50 a square foot and are rarely used in basement remodelling, but if you want the best, this is what you use.

Less expensive, and generally more suitable for home panelling, are the prefinished, random-grooved, hardwood veneer panels costing anywhere from 50¢ to $1 a square foot, depending on the species.

Unlike the simulated-woodgrain panels, real wood veneer will vary slightly in color and grain pattern. Stand the panels up around the room and shuffle them until you find the most attractive sequence, then number them on the back. Put the best panels on the wall facing the entrance to the room. If there are any mismatched panels, either take them back and exchange them or use them in areas where they won't be noticed.

Although they are not affected by humidity as much

as the hardboards are, all of these solid plywood panels should be allowed to adjust to room temperature and humidity for at least 48 hours before they are used. Stand them loosely against the wall so the air can circulate around them.

Gypsumboard

For basement walls that are to be painted or papered, inexpensive gypsumboard panelling may be the best answer. Also called "plasterboard" or "drywall", it is a rigid, fireproof panelboard made of gypsum or plaster sandwiched between two layers of heavy paper. Priced at about 12¢ a square foot, it is among the cheapest of the wall-panelling materials.

The heavy, rigid panels are awkward to handle, however. A 4' x 8' panel of ³⁄₈" gypsumboard weighs something over 45 pounds; ½" gypsumboard weighs about 60 pounds. And since the panels can't be bent, it may be difficult or impossible to get them down the basement stairs.

Gypsumboard is the only panelling material that can provide a completely smooth wall surface with invisible joints. Panel edges are tapered so they can be taped and filled with special jointing compound. For instructions on the use of gypsumboard, see Page 67.

Vinyl-faced Gypsumboard Although not ordinarily stocked by building supply stores, gypsumboard panels faced with a very tough, yet decorative, vinyl plastic sheet are widely used in offices and other commercial buildings. Completely waterproof and washable, they come in many colors, in burlap and other fabric textures and as well in simulated-woodgrains.

Canadian brands include Westroc Vinylboard, Sheetrock Textone, and Domtar Vinyl-Kote. These are available through a building supply dealer for approximately 40¢ a square foot, or about $13 for a 4' x 8' panel. Matching mouldings are available.

Solid Lumber Panelling

Although 4' x 8' panelboards are generally cheaper and easier to use, some people prefer the appearance and authenticity of solid lumber panelling. Prices run from about 35¢ to $1.50 a square foot.

Most panelling lumber is applied vertically. This requires horizontal framing supports about every 24" to provide at least four nailing points between the floor and the ceiling. (See Page 40.)

If square-edged lumber such as barnboard is to be used, the wall should first be covered with black building paper (see above) otherwise the polyethylene vapor barrier will show through the gaps between the boards. Panelling lumber is usually produced with a tongue-and-groove, V-joint edge, however, so that no gaps will show between the boards and they will be locked together to produce a flat, level wall.

The *back* of each board should be given a coat of shellac, varnish, or other sealer before being put up, to prevent warping from the uneven absorption of moisture. Cut all the boards $3/8''$ shorter than the actual wall height, and leave the gap at the bottom to be covered by the baseboard moulding.

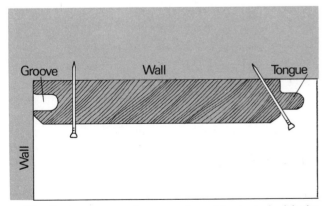

The first tongue-and-groove board is started with the grooved edge against the end wall, where it is nailed through the face as close to the end wall as possible. The other edge of the board is nailed through the tongue at an angle, and the nails are driven home with a nail set to avoid damaging the edge of the board with the hammer. These nails will be hidden inside the groove of the next board when it is pushed in place.

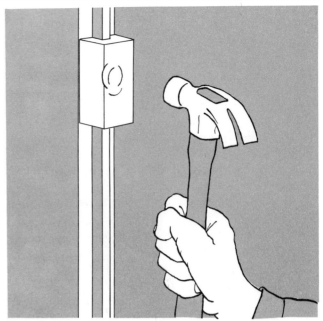

Using the grooved edge of a scrap piece of the panelling lumber to protect the tongue, tap each board in place before nailing... but not too tight. Leave a gap of about $1/16''$ between the boards to allow for expansion if the humidity increases.

Occasionally check the edge of the boards with a plumb line or a carpenter's level to make sure they are vertical. Slight adjustments can be made by opening or closing the joints as you go along. However, if the first board is badly out of plumb, trim the grooved edge with a saw before it is nailed in the corner.

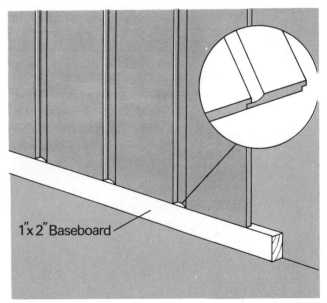

If regular baseboard moulding is used on top of deep V-joint, channel or beaded plank panelling, dust and dirt will fall behind the baseboard and be difficult to remove. A much neater arrangement is to nail a square-edge baseboard strip, such as a piece of 1x2, to the wall first, then butt the bottom of the panel boards to this. (The gap will be left at the top of the wall, to be covered by the ceiling moulding.)

Panelling

Horizontal Lumber Panelling

Shingles and Shakes

An attractive, rustic effect can be achieved by the use of various kinds of horizontal, exterior siding as interior wall panelling — the familiar, bevelled cedar siding, for instance, or the imitation log siding, a 1¼" thick, curved-face plank with a shiplap joint.

Siding comes in 8" and 10" widths in clear and construction grades. It is also available with either a smooth or rough-sawn face. Tongue-and-groove panelling, such as the clear cedar shown here, can also be applied horizontally.

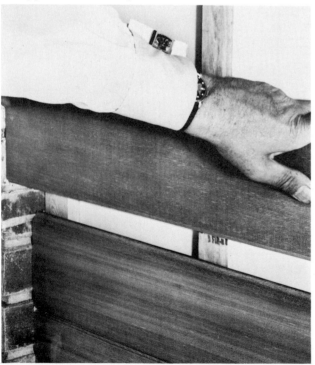

Although not usually thought of as an interior panelling material, the natural wood tones and texture of cedar shingles and shakes make these a very effective and unusual wall treatment that is also very easy to apply and maintain. Shingles are used more often than shakes because of their smoother finish and more delicate scale. They are also easier to apply.

For interior use, #3 or #4 grade shingles are quite satisfactory. They are available in 16", 18" and 24" lengths. The amount of wall coverage depends on the exposure of the shingles — how much of each shingle projects below the course above. This is usually just slightly less than half the length of the shingle. With this exposure, each bundle of shingles should cover about 40 square feet of wall.

Shingles can be fastened directly to the wall with nails, staples or panel adhesive. If the wall surface won't take nails, you can fasten the shingles to 1x2 nailing strips fastened horizontally to the wall by nailing through to the studs. The nailing strips should be spaced evenly from floor to ceiling, separated the same distance as the desired exposure of the shingles.

To determine the number of courses required, divide the distance between the top of the baseboard and the ceiling by the amount of shingle exposure. This is not likely to come out even, however, so you will have to reduce the shingle exposure enough to make up the difference.

Let's say your wall is exactly 96" from floor to ceiling. Subtracting 4" for the baseboard leaves 92" Dividing this by a shingle exposure of 8" (for 16" shingles) works out to 11½ courses, so you will need 12 courses. This gives you a shingle exposure of 7⅝" (92" ÷ 12).

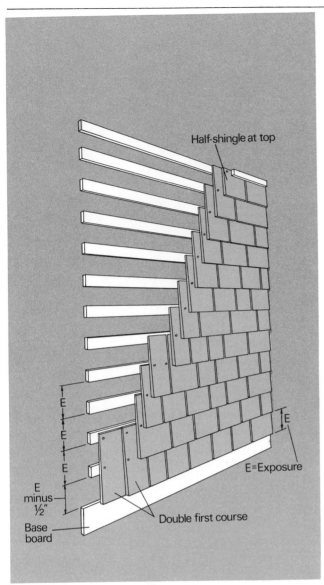

Half-shingle at top

E = Exposure

E
E
E
E minus ½"
Base board

Double first course

Applying Panelling

All panelling materials made from wood — and that includes hardboard, softboard, plywood and lumber — expand and contract with changes in humidity. Allowance must be made for this when cutting and applying panelling, otherwise it will warp and buckle during damp weather.

Panelling should be allowed to adjust to household humidity for two or three days before it is put up. In the case of panelboards, this is best done by standing them against the wall on their long edge so that the air can circulate around them. Lumber can be piled flat, with the layers separated by wood strips.

It is recommended that hardboard panels, which are most susceptible to humidity changes, be pre-expanded by wetting the backs of the panels thoroughly about 48 hours before use.

Panelling should never be cut to fit tightly between the floor and ceiling. It should be about ½" short, so that a gap can be left to allow for expansion; this will be hidden by the moulding.

Handling and Cutting All prefinished panelling materials should be handled carefully to avoid scratching the finish. *Lift* panels off a pile, don't slide them. Watch the corners; they break easily.

A simple workbench made of two sawhorses and two 2x6 or 2x8 planks at least 8' long will make it easier to mark and cut 4'x8' panelboards.

As shown in the illustration, the first nailing strip should be spaced above the baseboard the distance of the shingle exposure less ½" (this allows the first course to overhang the baseboard by ½"). The succeeding nailing strips are spaced just the exposure distance apart.

The first course of shingles along the bottom of the wall is a double course — two layers of shingles. (This is necessary to give the first course the same angle to the wall as the succeeding courses.) Be sure they overlap the baseboard by about ½".

The next course is applied as shown, with the lower end of each shingle placed to cover the nails in the course below. The bottom edges don't have to be perfectly even; a slightly ragged edge looks a lot better.

The last course at the top of the wall will consist of half-shingles. A batten strip or cove moulding can be applied to make a neater edge, if desired.

Cedar doesn't need any finish at all, but a slight darkening or mellowing of the natural color can be expected. However, any clear sealer, varnish, stain or paint can be used.

Panelling

If you use a handsaw or a table saw, both of which cut on the *down*stroke, lay the panels face up when cutting. If you use a portable power saw or a radial-arm saw, which cut on the *up*stroke, place the panel face side down and put newspapers underneath the panel to prevent the face from getting scratched.

When it is necessary to plane the edge of a plywood panel, plane from the ends toward the middle; don't plane straight along to the far end or you will chip off some of the face veneer. Hardboard, however, can be planed full-length without damaging the ends.

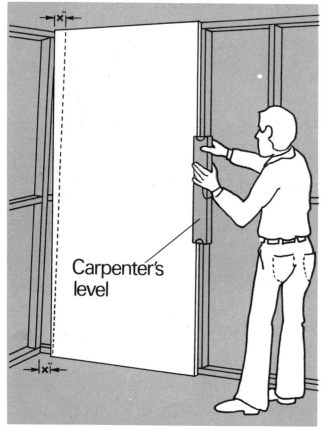

Carpenter's level

If your framing has been carefully built, with the corners square and plumb and a stud centred every 4', your panelling will go up quickly and easily. Simply start in a corner and continue around the room.

If the corner is not plumb, then you will have to trim the edge of the first panel to make it fit. Slide the panel into the corner, check the other edge with a level, then note any gap between the panel and the end wall. If the gap forms a straight line, simply mark this on the panel as shown above, then saw or plane off the waste. Succeeding panels on this wall will then fit plumb without any further trimming — until you get to the last panel, which will have to be trimmed if the end wall is not plumb.

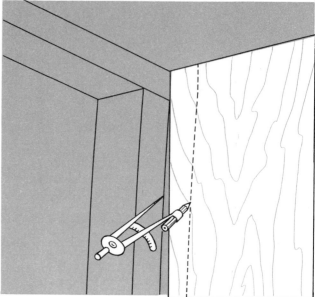

If the gap between the first panel and the end wall is curved or wavey rather than straight, you will have to mark on the panel the areas to be cut off. You can either do this freehand, if you have a good eye, or use a compass as shown above.

To complete the wall you will probably need a part panel. The easiest way to cut this is to take at least four measurements from the last full panel to the end wall as shown below.

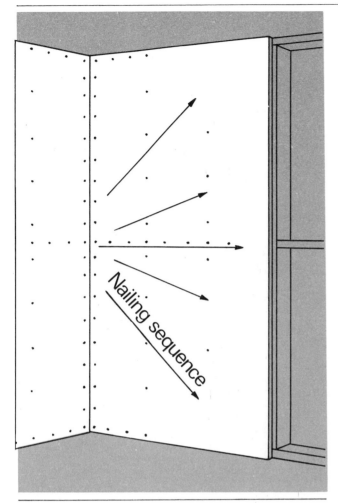

Nailing sequence

Nailing

Special, colored panel nails with needle points are recommended for use with hardboard or other finished panelboards. They should be spaced every 6″ along the panel edges and every 12″ along the intermediate studs and girts. Nail the joint edge first, then work across the panel as shown above. Don't nail around the outside of the panel first; this can cause the centre to buckle.

You will find that the V-grooves in simulated-plank panelling are spaced to fall on 16″ centres so that the nails can be hidden in the grooves.

Be careful not to dent the face of the panel with the hammer. Colored nails should just be driven flush with the face; plain steel nails should be countersunk with a nail set and then filled using a colored wax stick or an ordinary crayon that matches the panel. To avoid making too large a hole, use a nail set with a tip no larger than the head of the nail.

Panels should not be butted tightly together. Allow about the thickness of a dime between them for expansion. A couple of panel nails driven lightly into the stud at the edge of the panel will provide a convenient spacing gauge. Remove the nails after the next panel has been nailed in place.

To hide the expansion gap left between panel edges, spray the vapor barrier behind the joint with flat black paint or cover it with a strip of masking tape, before the panels are applied.

Adhesives

Panelling must be nailed to any wall that is insulated and covered with a vapor barrier, but it can be applied to all other walls with panel adhesive. This is more costly than nailing, but it is recommended for any finished panelboard with a smooth face where nails would show.

Panel adhesives come in a cartridge that fits the standard, inexpensive caulking gun. The adhesive is applied in a continuous bead or in 6″ strips. Where two panels meet on a stud, a zigzag line of adhesive will be needed.

Support the bottom of the panel on a scrap of wood to hold it clear of the floor while you press it gently against the adhesive on the studs. (Some experts recommend pulling the panel away from the studs again for a few minutes to let the adhesive dry a bit.) When in place, nail the top and bottom edges of the panel to the framing. If any edges spring out at the butt joint between the panels, nail a small block of wood over the joint as a temporary clamp until the adhesive sets.

Panelling

Walls Over Eight Feet High

A high basement can present a problem when it comes to finishing the walls with 4' x 8' panelboard materials. (There is no difficulty, of course, if you are using lumber panelling, although lengths over 8' will be more expensive.)

One solution is to put up a suspended ceiling (see Page 78) and hang it below the 8' level.

If the ceiling is only a few inches over 8' high, another simple solution is to use a filler strip along the bottom of the panel and cover it with a deep baseboard. Measure 8' down from the top of the wall and centre nailing girts between the studs at that point (see illustration below). Apply the 8' panel and the filler strips, leaving a gap of about ½" at the bottom. Baseboard moulding is available up to 3½" wide. If needed, a wider baseboard can be made out of clear finishing lumber by rounding the top edge with a plane.

A similar treatment can be used to place a filler strip along the top of the wall, but in this case two strips of moulding will probably be required to hide the joints, as shown in the illustration on the right. Since the filler strip will show, it will look better if it contrasts with the wall panelling.

Where the ceiling is more than a few inches higher than 8', it may be better to create a wainscot along the lower part of the wall, as shown in the illustration at the bottom, right. The wainscot should be at least 24" high and panelled with a different material or painted to contrast with the wall above it. The wainscot is usually made darker than the rest of the wall to hide chair marks. A decorative moulding is used to cover the joint.

The wainscot treatment also makes the ceiling appear lower.

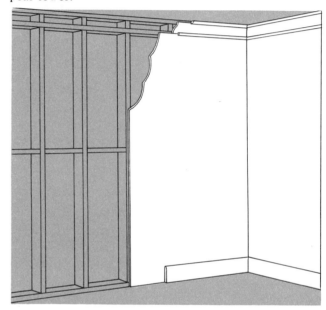

12 Drywall Panelling

Gypsumboard or drywall panelling is the best material to use if you want to paint or paper the walls of your basement rooms. It is also the least expensive of the panelling materials.

Aside from the fact that gypsumboard panels are heavy and inflexible, which may make them difficult to get downstairs, they are not at all difficult to apply. Any handyman capable of finishing a basement to the point of panelling will have no trouble putting up drywall and finishing all the joints to provide a smooth, unbroken wall surface.

Gypsumboard is available in 4' widths, 8' to 14' long. Professional drywall applicators use the longer lengths horizontally on the walls because they go up faster and have less joints to fill, but unless your walls are more than 8'2" high you will find it a lot easier to use 4' x 8' panels and apply them vertically, like the other panelboards we have discussed.

Gypsumboard panels come in $3/8''$, $1/2''$, and $5/8''$ thicknesses. The $3/8''$ panels are the lightest and easiest to handle (a 4' x 8' panel weighs about 47 pounds) but it is only pennies cheaper than the $1/2''$ thickness, which makes a much stronger wall. A full sheet of $1/2''$ gypsumboard weighs about 60 pounds and, while it can be managed by one person, it is easy for two.

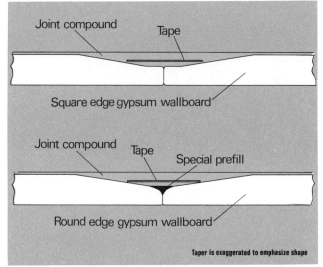

Taper is exaggerated to emphasize shape

The long edges of the gypsumboard panels are tapered slightly to provide space for taping and filling the joints. The most common type has a square edge,

but another type, with a rounded edge, is also available. This makes a stronger, smoother joint, but the deep groove formed by the rounded edge requires a separate application of a special, fast-setting filling compound and then standard joint compound to complete the joint. Square-edge panels, on the other hand, can be finished with one joint compound.

Gypsumboard panels are measured, fitted and applied much like the other panelboards (see Pages 63 to 66). All joints should be perfectly plumb and fall on the centre of a stud. Avoid joining panels at the edge of a door or window, however, since this is where cracks are most likely to occur. Instead, cut out a panel to fit over the opening, as shown in the photograph above.

Drywall panels are easy to cut. Most cuts are made with a straightedge and a razor knife. The first cut is made through the face paper and partly into the gypsum core, which can now be broken by snapping it back along the scored line. The break is completed by cutting through the paper on the back of the panel. The cut edges can be smoothed with coarse sandpaper wrapped around a hand-sized wooden block.

Where angle cuts are required to fit around a doorway or other opening, use a handsaw to make the short cut, then complete as described above.

Drywall Panelling

Fastening

Gypsumboard panels can be fastened to the framing with adhesive, nails or screws. Nailing is probably most convenient for the home handyman. Use 1¼″ annular, ringed nails, spaced 8″ apart along the framing. You will need about half a pound of nails for every 10′ of wall.

There should be a ½″ space between the bottom of the panel and the floor. Use a wedge or block to hold the panel to the ceiling while it is being nailed. Begin nailing at the centre of the panel and work outwards to the edges, holding the panel firmly against the studs. Drive each nail straight in, not at an angle, and not closer than ³/₈″ from the edge.

There is one important trick in nailing gypsumboard panelling. When the nail has been driven flush with the face, give it one more blow with the hammer to depress it below the surface and form a smooth crater on the paper face. But be careful not to cut through the paper or crumble the gypsum core. If you do, the nail will not hold and another one should be driven in about 2″ away.

Do not attempt to countersink gypsumboard nails with a nail set.

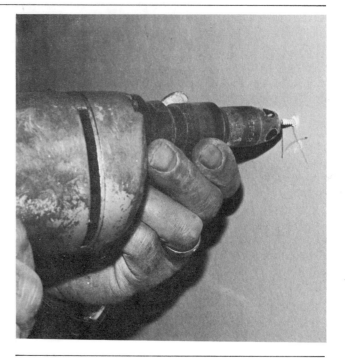

Screws

Professional drywall applicators generally use screws, which have twice the holding power of the ringed nails and can be spaced farther apart — 16″ instead of 8″. Drywall screws have a Phillips head (X-shaped slot) and should be driven with a special screw-gun with a slip clutch head that can be set to drive the screw exactly the right depth below the surface without breaking the paper face. These electric screwdrivers can be obtained from any tool rental shop along with a supply of 1¼″ Type W (for wood) drywall screws. (If you have metal studs, you will need 1″ Type S drywall screws.)

Adhesives

Although it is more trouble than nailing, the application of gypsumboard panels by means of adhesive (plus a few nails) has several advantages. It reduces nail-popping problems, is twice as strong, bridges minor framing irregularities and is unaffected by moisture, an important consideration in basement construction.

Several brands of drywall panel adhesive are available in standard, 30-ounce cartridges that fit the familiar caulking gun. A continuous, ³/₈″ bead of adhesive is squeezed out down the centre of the studs to within 6″ of the ends. When two panels will join on

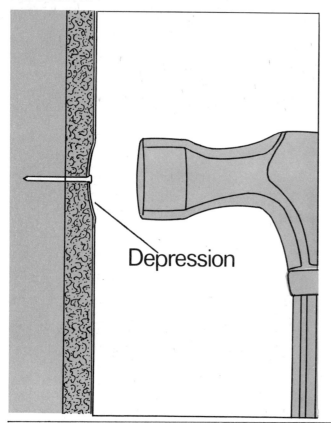

Depression

a stud, however, the adhesive is applied in a zig-zag line down the stud so that both panels will be bonded.

Adhesive is not required along the horizontal framing members.

Apply the panel as soon as possible after the adhesive has been applied. Support it on a wood block at the bottom, then fasten with nails spaced every 16" on both edges. Nails are not required along the top or bottom or on intermediate studs. Press the panel firmly in place on all studs to spread the adhesive.

Joint Treatment

The tapered edges of gypsumboard panels permit the joints to be taped and filled level with the wall surface. Properly done, the joints will be invisible even on a painted wall. The procedure is not difficult.

Most of the gypsumboard sold by retail lumberyards and building supply dealers is the square-edge type (see Page 67). But if your panels have a rounded edge, the first step is to fill the resulting deep joint crack with a special, fast-setting compound such as CGC Durabond 90, Domtar RE Filler or Westroc Rapidfil. These harden chemically within 90 minutes; after that the filling and taping procedure is the same as for the tapered, square-edge panels, described below.

Joints are filled with an all-purpose joint compound, either powdered or ready-mixed, and a perforated, fibre-reinforced paper tape that is tapered at the edges to form a smooth surface. Most of the powdered joint compounds are now asbestos-free, but not the ready-mixed compounds. They should be wet-sanded or wiped with a damp sponge to avoid getting any of the dust in the air.

You will need about 5 pounds of powdered joint compound or ½-gallon of ready-mixed plus 30' of tape for every 10' of wall

Powdered joint compound should be allowed to stand for about 30 minutes and then re-mixed before it is used. It will be thin when it is first mixed, but will thicken when it's ready to use. Mix no more than enough to cover one day's work.

Because all joint compounds shrink when they dry, it is necessary to apply three separate coats to obtain a smooth joint that will be invisible when painted.

Flat Joints

Flat wall joints can be filled most easily with an 11" plasterer's trowel. You will also need a hawk, which is just a square piece of metal or plywood with a handle in the centre. It is used to hold a quantity of joint filler to be picked up by the trowel as needed. You can make a hawk out of a 14" square piece of ¼" plywood nailed or screwed through the centre to a 5" length of 1" dowel.

Spread a ribbon of joint compound about 3" wide down the centre of the hawk as shown here, placing it so that the hawk is evenly balanced in your hand.

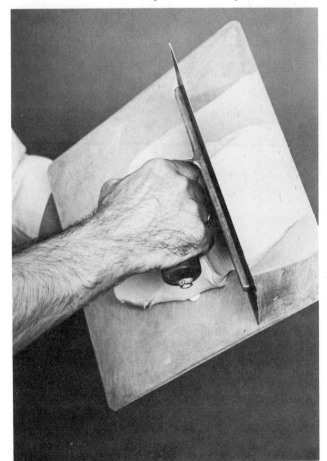

Pick up a portion of joint compound from the hawk with the trowel. You will quickly discover the right quantity to give you a full stroke with the trowel.

Drywall Panelling

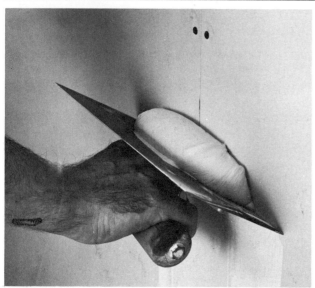

The trowel is swept up the joint in a continuous motion, forcing the compound into the 5″ wide depression formed by the tapered edges of the panels. The filled area shows as a dark strip below the trowel in this photograph.

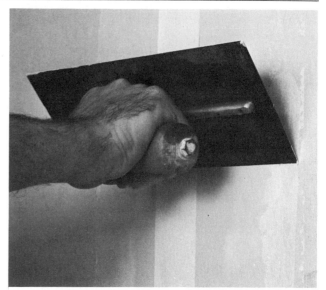

Immediately apply a thin coat of joint compound over the tape to bed it firmly. Work from the centre of the wall, first up, then down, to avoid wrinkles in the tape. Don't waste time trying to make this first layer of joint compound perfectly smooth; it's supposed to be rough.

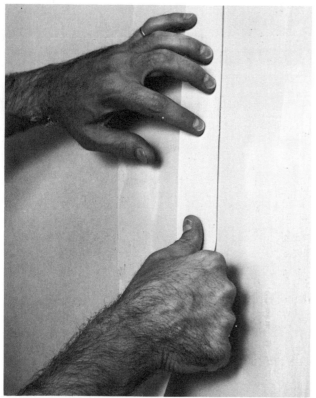

Immediately lay the joint tape in the wet compound with the centre fold toward you, as if you were looking at the pages of a book. Use a continuous strip the length of the wall to avoid joints or overlaps.

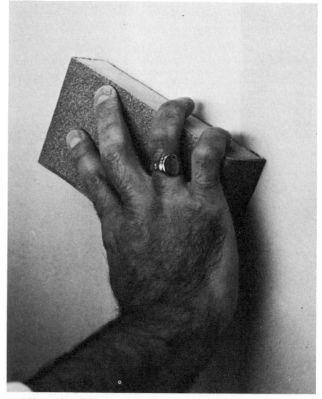

Allow the joint to dry thoroughly, at least 24 hours, preferably 48. Then sand lightly with #100 grit sandpaper on a wood block.

Use a damp sponge to remove sanding dust. If you have used a dry-mix joint compound that contains asbestos, use a wet sponge instead of sandpaper to smooth the joint.

A second coat, about 10″ wide, is applied like the first, allowed to dry, and then sanded or damp-sponged lightly. This coat will be also slightly rough when it dries. Imperfections will be covered by the third and last coat.

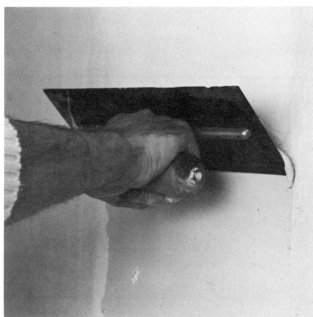

For the third coat use a wider portion of joint compound on the trowel so that it will spread just beyond the edges. Only a very thin layer is needed. Use a clean trowel to feather the edge of the joint, which will now be about 15″ wide. If properly applied it will dry with a smooth, even texture that matches the paper surface of the gypsumboard. No sanding or sponging should be needed.

Nail Depressions

The dimples that were formed when the nails were driven below the surface of the gypsumboard as described on Page 68 should be filled with joint compound in three steps at the same time as the wall joints are done.

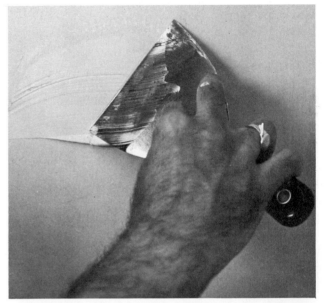

A 6″ putty knife is used to fill the nail depressions. First apply the joint compound over the nail with a sweep of the knife in one direction . .

. . . then wipe off the excess in the opposite direction. If you hear a metalic click when you wipe the putty knife over the dimple, stop and drive the nail home, then refill. (Your trowel can be used as a hawk to hold the joint compound when you are filling nail holes with a putty knife.)

Drywall Panelling

Inside Corners

The same principle of filling and taping is used for inside corner joints. Only two coats of compound are needed because these edges of the gypsumboard panels have usually been cut to fit and are therefore not tapered, so the compound will be thinner and there will be less shrinkage.

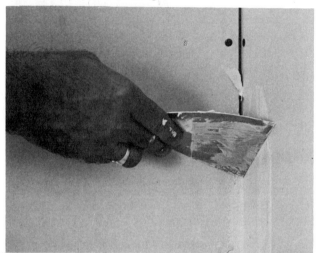

A flexible, 6″ putty knife is used to apply the joint compound to each side of the corner, using a dab of compound on the inside corner of the knife only. (Special drywall jointing knives with square-cut instead of curved edges are available. They make it easier to apply joint compound to one wall without it also squeezing out on the other wall, as is happening here.)

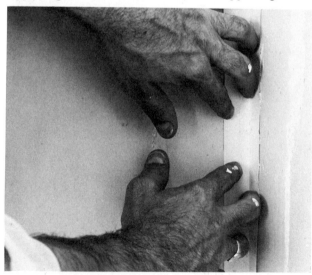

When a layer of compound has been applied to both sides of the corner, fold a strip of tape along its crease and press it in place in the corner.

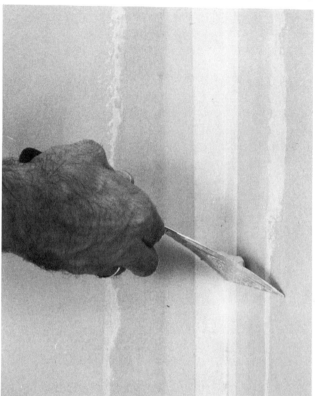

Put a little compound on one edge of the putty knife and spread it over each side of the tape, pressing it firmly in place.

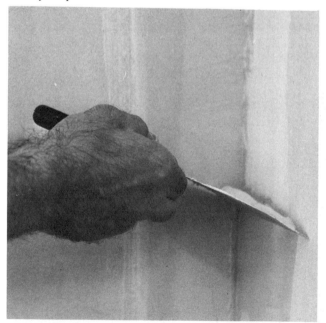

After the first application of compound has dried thoroughly, sand or wet-sponge lightly. Then apply a second and final coat of compound to both sides of the corner, feathering it out about 6″.

Outside Corners

Outside corner joints must be reinforced with metal corner bead to protect the gypsumboard from the inevitable blows it will receive from furniture, vacuum cleaners, ladders, etc.

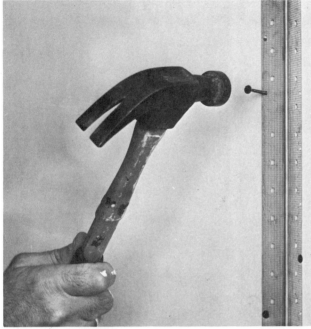

Metal corner bead is nailed over the outside corner joint. Nails should be spaced about 12″ apart and driven flush.

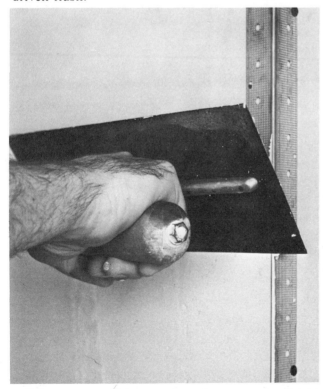

Joint compound is spread on the corner bead with one edge of the trowel resting on the bead and the other on the wall about 10″ back.

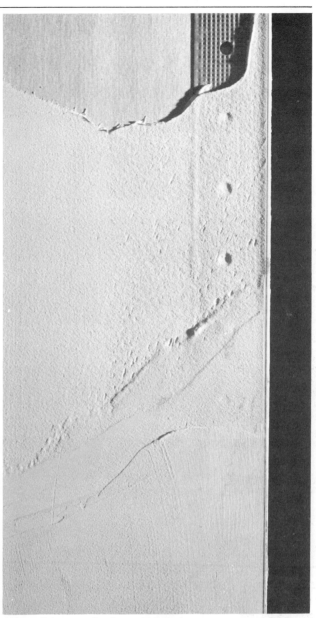

This photograph shows why three separate layers of compound are required to give a smooth joint finish. The first layer (top) is the thickest and shows small depressions when it dries and shrinks. The second layer, just below it, dries smoother, but still shows an uneven surface when it dries. The third layer, on the bottom, has an even texture and is perfectly flat.

Finishing Drywall

If you want to paint your drywall panelling, use a latex primer or a latex paint that is self-priming. A latex primer should even be used under an alkyd or other oil-based paint.

But if you want to paper the wall, first seal it with a good enamel undercoat. When this is dry, apply a coat of wall size. This will allow the new, dry-strippable papers to be removed easily without damaging the paper face of the gypsumboard panels.

13 Ceilings

There are several different ways to put up a ceiling, depending on the height of the room, how you want to use it, and the style you wish to achieve.

If you plan an informal living or recreation area, the ceiling can be finished with acoustic tile that is inexpensive, helps to absorb sounds, and is easy to maintain. A casual, tiled-ceiling effect can also be achieved with large, prefinished hardboard or plywood panels that have been scored to represent 12" x 12" square tiles.

Where there is enough height, you can put up a split-level ceiling with a raised centre section surrounded by concealed lights, or a dropped ceiling with recessed pot lights over the bar.

If you want a more formal room with a painted or textured plaster ceiling, put up gypsumboard panels and finish the joints as described on Pages 67 to 71. The only difference in the procedure for panelling a ceiling is that it takes two people to hold up and attach the heavy panels. A T-shaped support about 2" longer than the distance from the floor to the ceiling, made from 2x4 lumber, can be used to hold up the panel, but it still takes two people to put it there.

Most basement living areas, however, use tiled ceilings. There are two ways these can be applied. One is to nail 1x3 strapping across the joists, then staple the tiles to this. The other is to suspend a metal grid from the joists and drop in 2'x2' or 2'x4' ceiling panels.

One advantage of a suspended ceiling is that it will cover pipes, brackets, heating ducts, beams and other projections without the trouble of having to build around them. It is also a good way to lower a high ceiling.

The disadvantage of a suspended ceiling is that it requires a minimum of 4" of space below the joists, which you don't always have in a basement. It is also a little more expensive that a strapped ceiling.

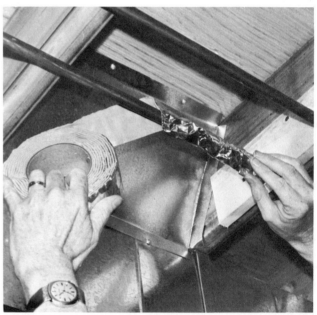

Regardless of which system you use, before you put up the ceiling, wrap overhead cold-water pipes with insulation to prevent condensation that would drip on to your ceiling tiles. Special insulation tape for this purpose is sold at most hardware and building supply stores. Some is foil-backed plastic foam, as shown above; some is fibreglass with a kraft paper backing.

It's a good idea, too, to leave the final placement of lighting fixtures until you know the layout of the ceiling tiles, so that the fixtures can be located to fit the tile pattern. However, the rough wiring should be put in before the ceiling is covered.

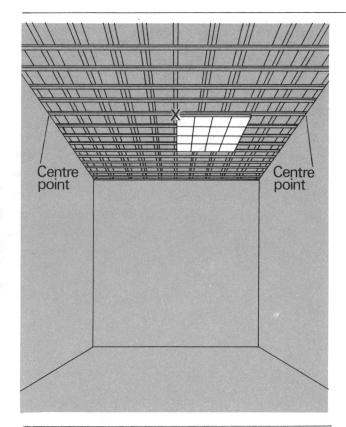

Centre point   Centre point

Panelboard

The easiest and cheapest type of ceiling tiles to put up are the prefinished 4′ x 4′ hardboard panels, grooved to give the appearance of 12″ square tiles. These panels come with embossed and textured finishes in plain white as well as metallic-flecked.

The 4′ x 4′ panels are fastened to 1x3 strapping nailed across the joists. To locate the starting point, find the mid-point of the two walls that are parallel to the joists. Snap a chalk line between these two points to mark the joists, then centre the first length of strapping over this line. Nail the rest of the strapping parallel to this one, spaced 12″ apart, centre to centre.

Now measure and mark the mid-point of the first length of strapping you put up. This is where you will start your first ceiling panel. But before you do, you will have to nail short lengths of 1x3 to the joists between the strapping every 4′ to support the edges of the panels.

Tiles

More commonly used are the prefinished softboard ceiling tiles in 12″ squares with tongue-and-groove edges. These are also nailed or stapled to 1x3 strapping, but the procedure is slightly different because the small tiles are not self-aligning as the large panels are.

A little mathematics is required to find the correct location for the strapping, which is always nailed at right-angles to the ceiling joists, of course.

The tiles are 12″ square, so if the width of the room is an exact number of feet, the location of the tiles is simple. You would simply start on one side and continue across the room. More likely, however, the ceiling measurement will have a few inches left over. A border less than 5″ wide is both wasteful and unattractive, but there's a simple way to avoid this. Divide the room width by two. If the number of inches left over is less than 5, add 6″ to it, and that is the width of the border tiles on each side of the room.

Examples: Room width = 11′4″. Divide by two = 5′8″. Eight inches is an acceptable width for the border tiles.

Room width = 10′6″. Divide by two = 5′3″. Three inches is too narrow for a border strip, so add 6″, which gives you a border tile width of 9″.

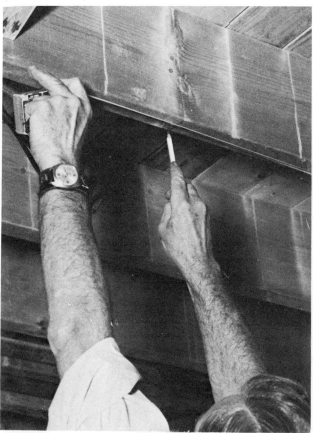

The first length of strapping is nailed flush to the wall framing with 2″ common nails. The *centre* of the next nailing strip is the width of the border tile from the wall plus ½″ allowance for the stapling flange of the tile. The succeeding lengths of strapping will be spaced exactly 12″ on centres from this one. Don't just measure from one length of strapping to the next. Even a slight error in each measurement can result in a large discrepancy by the time you reach the opposite wall. Instead, hook a measuring tape to the inside edge of the second length of strapping and mark the joist every 12″. Do this in at least four places across the ceiling and use these marks to line up the edges of succeeding strapping.

Ceilings

Check the level of the joists with a string drawn across them. Where necessary, put wood blocks or shingle shims under the strapping to level the ceiling.

(If your house is very old, you can get a lot of dust or other dirt in your hair and eyes when you start hammering on the ceiling. Some experts recommend stapling a sheet of polyethylene film under the joists before you put up the strapping.)

Warm air ducts and cold air returns usually run between the joists and don't get in the way of your ceiling, but the main warm air supply plenum is always located *below* the joists and will have to be boxed-in before the ceiling strapping is applied (see Page 47). Unless, that is, you're satisfied just to paint the plenum with flat white interior latex, which looks quite good and saves a great deal of work. (See photograph Page 47.)

(The wall panelling should be applied now, as described in Chapter 11, after the ceiling strapping has been put up and *before* the tiles are put on.)

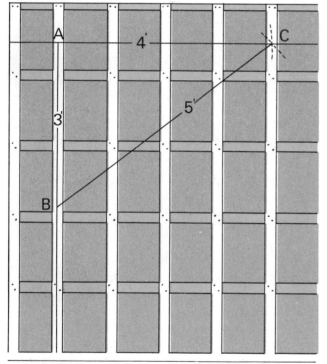

Squaring the Tiles

Before you can start with your first ceiling tile in the corner you will have to determine the width of the border tiles down the other two sides of the room. Measure this the same way you did the other border strips (Page 75). Mark this point A as shown in the illustration above.

If the walls of the room are parallel and perfectly square, you can simply start in the corner by cutting and applying the border tiles according to the measurements you have determined. It's best to check before you start, however; you'll be surprised how often you find the room is crooked.

To do this, snap a chalk line down the centre of the second nailing strip from the wall, starting at point A. (This will mark the edge of the border tiles.) If you have a large sheet of plywood or hardboard, you can use this as a square to mark the border tile line AC. Get someone to hold one edge of the panel along AB while you snap a chalk line along AC to the other end of the room, marking the border tile line on the strapping.

If you don't have anything large enough to give you an accurate right angle, use the 3-4-5 geometry trick. The distance between A and B is 3'. If you now use measuring tapes or lengths of string to measure exactly 4' from A and 5' from B, the point C where they intersect will give you an accurate right angle between AB and AC. (If you find that C falls between two nailing strips, fasten a short length of strapping across them temporarily and mark point C on this.)

Draw a string along AC to the other end of the room and mark all the nailing strips where it passes.

Applying the Tiles

Start applying the ceiling tiles in the corner. Use a razor knife and a straightedge to cut the border tiles, face up, leaving the flange edge to be stapled to the strapping. Apply a few border tiles along both walls, lining them up with the marks on the strapping and cutting each one to fit.

The ceiling will now go up quickly as you work out from the corner, applying the border tiles first, then filling in with full tiles. You will notice that only two edges of each tile are stapled to the strapping; the other two are held by the tongue-and-groove joint. Use a standard staple gun and $9/16''$ staples.

Leave roughed-in openings in the tile ceiling for lighting fixtures, which can then be framed in and installed to fit the tile pattern. (Recessed light fixtures are available in a 12'' x 12'' size with special adapter plates that fit between the strapping.)

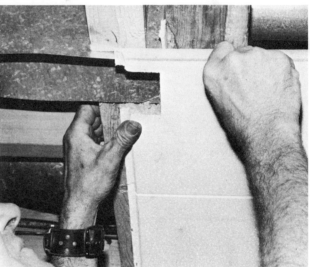

Where the ceiling outlets are already in place, as in the case of warm air ducts, cut the tiles to fit around them as shown.

Ceilings

Suspended Ceilings

If there are a lot of pipes, heating ducts, beams and other obstructions below the ceiling joists in your basement, and the joists are 8' or more above the floor, the best way to finish the ceiling is by putting in a suspended grid system with drop-in panels of decorative ceiling tile or translucent light screens. This is essentially the same system that you've seen in many commercial buildings, only lighter and easier to install.

Several different makes are available at building supply stores but they are all much the same. Most are steel but one grid system is made of white vinyl plastic. T-shaped main runners are hung from the ceiling joists on short lengths of wire, metal or plastic strips. Cross members simply snap into the main runners, creating a suspended framework of 2' x 2' or 2' x 4' openings into which pre-cut ceiling panels are dropped. The loose panels make it easy to reach pipes or wiring above the ceiling at any time. The metal grid has a factory-applied, white enamel finish. White ceiling panels are available in a number of textures and surface patterns.

A 2' x 4' grid is a little cheaper and easier to put up than a 2' x 2' grid, because it uses less metal, but the smaller squares look better in a small room.

Installing the Grid

The only trick in putting up a suspended ceiling is finding the right position for the grid lines. The width and length of the room will never be an exact multiple of the grid size — 2' or 4' — so you'll have to centre the grid framework to provide equal spacing on each side of the ceiling, and cut panels to fit these borders. If the borders are less than half a panel, it will be better to eliminate one row to make wider borders of between a half-panel and a full-panel.

One way to determine this is to draw a floor plan of the room on tissue paper at a scale of ¼" to 1' and lay this over ¼" squared paper with parallel pencil lines drawn every 1" to indicate 4' grid lines or every ½" to indicate 2' grid lines. (Note on the floor plan which way the ceiling joists go; remember that the main grid lines will run at right-angles to the joists.)

This plan can also be used to calculate how much grid material and the number of panels you will need.

Another way to find the size of the border panels is to work it out mathematically, very much as was done for the 12" ceiling tiles on Page 75. The formula is

changed to suit the larger size of the suspended ceiling panels, however.

Change the room dimensions to inches, then divide by the panel size (24" or 48"). If it goes in evenly, the border will be a full panel. If there is anything left over, add the size of one panel (24" or 48") and divide by 2. The result is the width of the border panel required on each side of the ceiling.

Example: Wall length: 14'9" = 177". Divided by 24 = 7 with 9" left over. 9" + 24" = 33", divided by 2 = 16½", which is the width of the border panels.

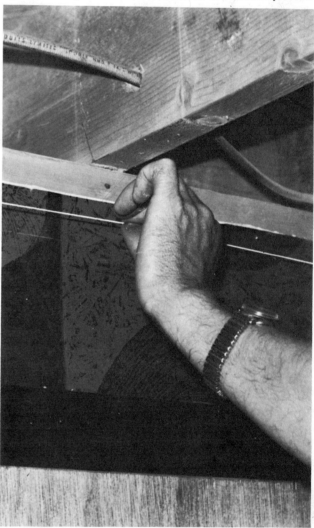

The next step is to put up the L-shaped wall strip, the bottom edge of which must be at least 4" below the lowest ceiling projection to allow space to insert or remove the ceiling panels. Mark this point on the wall and use a string level and chalk line to mark the finished ceiling height around the four walls. (It isn't a good idea to measure up from the floor because it may not be level.)

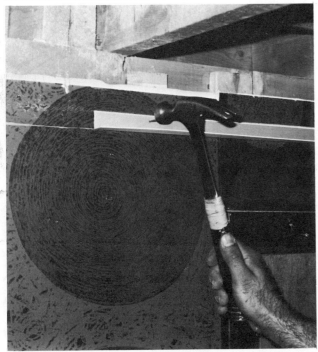

Attach the wall strip along this line around the four walls, nailing through to every second stud. Note that the bottom of the wall strip is level with the chalk mark. (Obviously this strip cannot be put up until the walls have been panelled!)

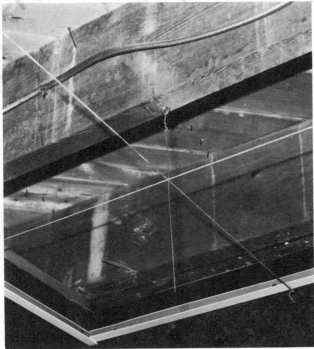

The border widths that you have determined previously are now marked on the wall strip and strings drawn tightly from wall to wall to mark the location of the borders. Check to make sure they form a 90° angle where they intersect; adjust if necessary. Fasten a screw-eye to the ceiling where the strings intersect and attach a length of wire. This will support the first line of main runners. Install additional wire hangers every 4' across the string line.

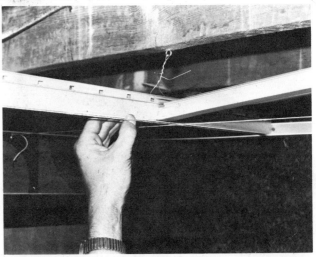

After the main runner has been supported parallel to and level with the string by additional wire hangers, the other main runners are put up at 4' intervals. The 4' cross-tees are now placed between the main runners, with their tab ends slipped into the appropriate connector slots.

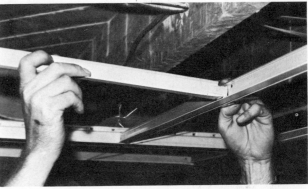

Additional cross-tees are now connected at right-angles to create the 2' x 4' ceiling grid. Only the main runners, 4' apart, are supported by the ceiling wires.

Prefinished ceiling panels are simply lifted and dropped into the openings of the suspended grid.

Other types of suspended ceiling system may work slightly differently from the Domtar/Donn *system shown here, but the basic principles are the same.*

Ceilings

False Beams

If you want to give your recreation room the rustic look of an old English inn or an Early Canadian farmhouse, you can make your own hand-hewn "timbers" out of inexpensive plastic foamboard ... the common white insulation board often mistakenly called Styrofoam.

The sides of the beams are made out of 2" x 2" strips cut from the 2" foamboard. These are glued to the underside of the 1" face strip to make a U-shaped beam 3" thick. Any of the common white resin adhesives can be used. Weight the beams and allow 24 hours to dry.

The foamboard comes in 4' x 8' sheets in various thicknesses. You'll need both 1" and 2" thicknesses. The 1" sheet is cut into strips the width of your beams. If you make this 6 7/8" you'll get seven strips out of one sheet without any waste, or a total of 56 lineal feet. These strips make the face of your beams. Foamboard is easily cut with a razor knife or a saw-toothed bread knife.

Use a long, razor-sharp knife to round the edges and take out slightly curved slices resembling the cuts made by an adze or an axe. Long, straight, V-shaped cuts that remove a thin wedge of plastic will simulate cracks and checks in the wood. Paint the finished beam with a dark brown shingle stain or a flat latex paint. Attach to the ceiling with a few dabs of panel adhesive.

14 Stairways

The position of the stairway will have been taken into consideration when you drew up your basement floor plans (see Page 17), since it plays a large part in determining how the area can best be used. The stairway is almost always closed-in just the way it is; very rarely is it worthwhile to change it in any way.

However, the space under the stairway can be put to very practical use — for storage, at the very least, but often for built-in seating, desk space, a bar or other useful functions. Where there is access to the space under the stairs, as in the example shown in the photographs below, the side of the stairway can simply be closed in. In other situations it may be necessary to put cupboard doors in the side of the closed-in staifway. In either case, the framing is simple and straight-forward.

If the stair treads are closed in by the stringer (the board that supports the side of the stairs), then the panelling is simply applied over them as shown in the photographs on the left. The edge is finished with a molding strip. Where the stair treads extend over an open stringer, however, as in the illustration above, the panelling must be notched to fit around the edge of the treads.

An alternative use of the space under an open stairway is shown below, where built-in seating and bookshelves have been constructed in the stairway alcove.

15 Doors

The most important step in hanging a door is building the rough framing properly (see Page 44). If this is plumb, square and the right size, hanging the door will be easy.

Hollow core, plywood doors are generally preferred for interior use today. They are much less expensive and easier to handle than solid wood doors, though these are available. The standard thickness is $1\frac{3}{8}''$. The most common height is 6'8'', but 6'6'' doors can be purchased. Widths range from 1' to 3' in 2'' steps — 2'6'' is the most popular size.

Pre-hung doors are also available, complete with hinges and jamb, ready to be installed in the rough-framed opening. Latch sets are not included, however.

The rough-framed opening should be 2'' wider than the door and $1\frac{1}{2}''$ higher to allow for the thickness of the jamb and the spacing around the door, including the normal $\frac{1}{2}''$ gap at the bottom. If you intend to lay carpet up to the door, this space should be increased accordingly.

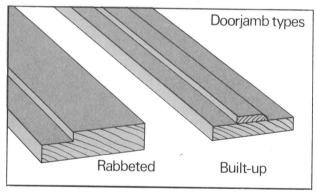

Doorjamb types

Rabbeted   Built-up

Framing

Although you can use any clear, finishing lumber to make a doorjamb, it is generally better to buy a jamb set — consisting of two matched pieces 7' long and one piece 3' long. Some jamb sets are made of $1\frac{1}{2}''$ x $5\frac{1}{2}''$ lumber rabbeted $\frac{1}{2}''$ x $1\frac{1}{4}''$ to form an integral doorstop. Less expensive sets made of $\frac{3}{4}''$ lumber require a separate set of doorstop moulding and are quite satisfactory for any interior use.

Doorjamb sets are normally available in $3\frac{1}{2}''$, $4\frac{1}{2}''$, 5'' and $5\frac{1}{2}''$ widths. Choose the size closest to the total

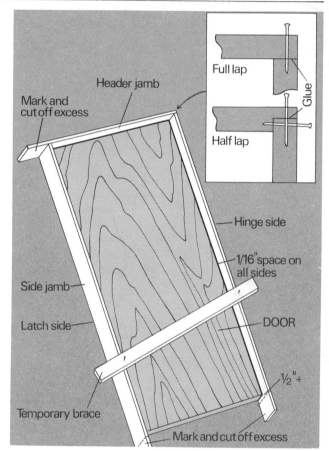

Full lap

Glue

Half lap

Mark and cut off excess

Header jamb

Hinge side

1/16" space on all sides

Side jamb

Latch side

DOOR

Temporary brace

$\frac{1}{2}''+$

Mark and cut off excess

thickness of your finished wall. A standard 2x4 frame wall with $\frac{1}{4}''$ panelling on both sides will be exactly 4'' thick. Use a $4\frac{1}{2}''$ jamb set and plane all three pieces down to $4\frac{1}{8}''$, bevelling the edges back about 10° as shown in the bottom illustration on the opposite page. This will provide a slightly projecting edge that will allow the casing frame to fit tightly around the doorway.

To assemble the doorjamb, use the door itself as the pattern. Lay it on the floor over top of a large piece of paper and place the three jamb pieces around it. Use pennies as spacers to give $\frac{1}{16}''$ clearance between the door and the jamb at both sides and the top. The header jamb should overlap the side jambs (a half-lap joint can be used, but be sure to allow for this when measuring the length of the side pieces).

Mark the cut-off points on the header and legs. Cut and re-assemble, gluing and nailing the header to the side pieces. Hold the legs at the bottom with a temporary brace.

Lift the assembled jamb off the door and place it in the rough-framed doorway. Check the width of the jamb; the bevelled edge should project about $1/16''$ on either side of the finished wall as shown in the illustration below. Press the hinge-side jamb tightly to the rough-framing and use a level to make sure it is perfectly plumb. Use wood shingle shims if necessary. The bottom of the jamb should be $1/8''$ above the finished floor.

Nail the hinge-side of the doorjamb to the rough framing with $2''$ finishing nails. The header and the other side can be left loose at this point.

Hanging the Door

If you intend to give the door a clear, woodgrain finish, before attaching the hinges examine it carefully to determine the best face. The best side of the door should face into the room. Doors are generally hung to open into the room, but this is a matter of choice, as is a left- or right-hand opening.

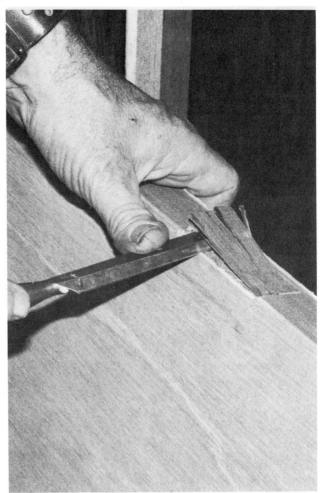

You will need one pair of $3''$x$3''$, loose-pin, butt hinges. These are normally set $6''$ from the top of the door and $9''$ from the bottom.

Place the hinge in position on the edge of the door and trace around it with a pencil, then cut along the line about $1/16''$ deep with a broad chisel. Or use a butt hinge marker as shown on the left. In either case, the waste wood must be removed to the depth of the hinge leaf with a chisel.

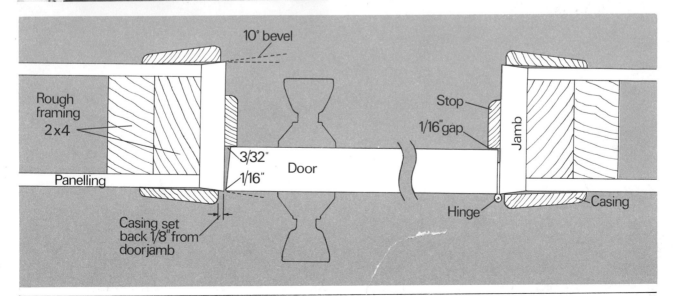

continued

Doors

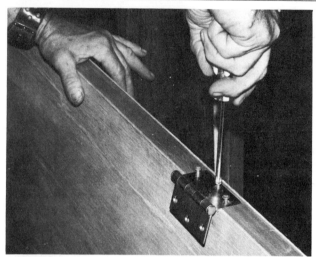

Use an awl or a centre-punch to start screw holes in the door, then attach the hinge with the screws provided.

Chisel out the waste wood as before, then use a nail to knock out the hinge pin so that the loose leaf can be screwed to the doorjamb (below).

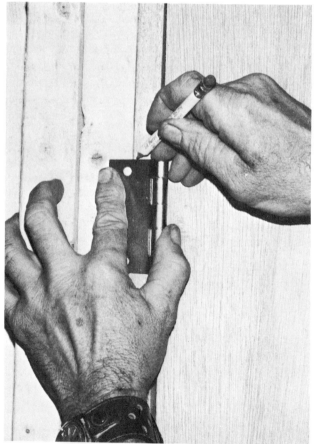

Put the door in place, supported on a wooden wedge to provide the required bottom clearance and a gap of $^1/_{16}''$ at the top. Use the loose hinge leaf to mark the position in the doorjamb (in this case on the left side of the door).

The door is now hung on its hinges by replacing the pins, and the jamb is nailed to the latch side of the doorway, using wood shingle shims to give a clearance of about $1/16''$ if the edge of the door has been planed to a slight bevel, as shown in illustration at the bottom of Page 83 or a clearance of $1/8''$ if the edge has not been bevelled.

Installing a Latch Set

Unless you want to be able to lock your basement room with a key, a simple "passage set" is all you will require for the door. If you want to be able to lock the door from the inside, get a "privacy set" with a locking button or lever on the inside knob.

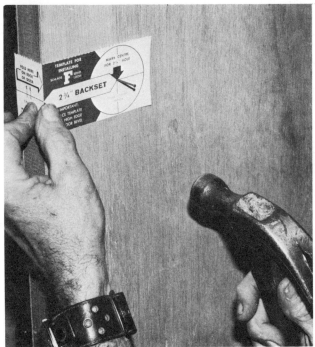

The door handle is normally placed 36'' above the floor. Your passage set will come with templates and instructions for fitting. The cardboard template shown here marks the centre point for drilling a $2 1/8''$ hole in the door. It is marked with a nail.

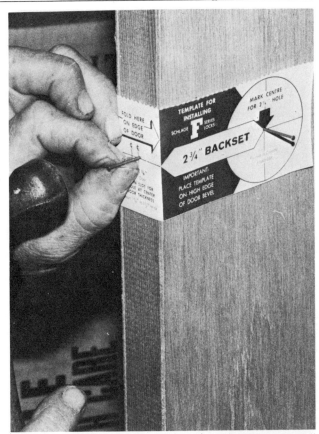

Another nail marks the centre point for drilling a $7/8''$ hole in the edge of the door for the latch bolt. Hollow plywood doors have a solid wood core at the point where handles and latches are normally located.

This special attachment can be used to drill large holes through the solid core of a door with a $3/8''$ electric drill. A small pilot bit in the centre guides the drum saw. When the bit protrudes on the other side, the drill is removed and started again on the other side. An old-fashioned brace and expansion bit works just as well, but must also be used on both sides to prevent chipping the veneer face.

A hole of the required size is then drilled in the edge of the door for the latch bolt. The bolt is put in place and the plate outlined in pencil as a guide to chiselling out the required recess with a 1'' chisel.

Doors

With the latch plate and bolt mechanism screwed in place, the handles are inserted and the escutcheon plates are fastened to the door.

The door is closed and the position of the latch is marked on the jamb. Note the shingle shim behind the jamb.

The latch plate is placed upside down on the jamb with the latch hole in line with the previous mark, and the outline is drawn on the jamb.

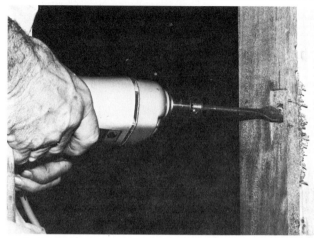

A chisel is used to cut a recess in the jamb to take the latch plate, and a 7/8″ hole is drilled in the centre to accommodate the bolt. The latch plate is then screwed in place.

Doorstop Moulding

Experience has shown that it is generally better to put the doorstop moulding in place after the latch set has been installed. Otherwise it may be necessary to remove and locate the stops to get the latch to seat properly.

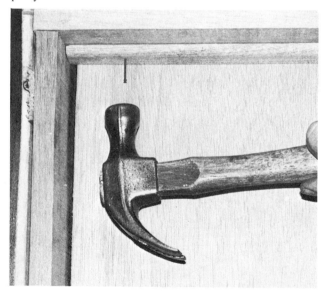

Cut a piece of stop moulding 1/16″ longer than the width of the opening and wedge this in place at the top of the door jamb. The stop should touch the door on the latch side, but be 1/16″ away from the door on the hinge side, providing enough space for the door to swing open without hitting the stop.

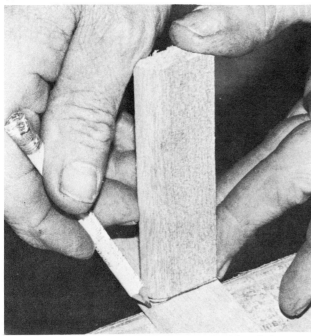

Put the stop moulding on the latch side of the door next. A coped joint is used to fit this piece of moulding to the piece already in place at the top of the door jamb. Use a piece of scrap moulding to mark the shape of the cut to be made on the side moulding.

A coping saw is used to cut the side stop moulding to size, following the outline described above.

Here's how the two pieces of moulding will now fit together. The top moulding is on the left, the side moulding is on the bottom. Both side pieces of stop moulding are cut in this way before they are nailed in place on the side jambs. Note that the stop moulding on the hinge side of the door must be set back $^1/_{16}''$ to leave space for the edge to swing open.

Casing

The door opening is finished off by framing it with casing moulding, mitered at the top two corners and set back $^1/_8''$ from the edge of the jamb, as shown in the illustration on Page 83. If a clear finish is to be applied, the casing should be made of the same wood as the door and the jamb, usually Philippine mahogany, or lauan. A number of different moulding shapes are available, but $^1/_2''$ x $3''$ lumber can be used to make a very simple casing.

16 Floors

Many people believe that a basement floor must be insulated to conserve heat and keep the rooms from feeling cold. The truth is that very little heat is lost through a basement floor. It is already well insulated by several feet of earth, and has, in fact, an effective insulation value of about R40 ... twice as much as the maximum presently required in ceilings!

There are two reasons why basements feel cold during the winter: lack of insulation in the walls, particularly above ground level, and, in the case of homes heated with warm air, the lack of a cold air return vent on the basement floor (see Page 30).

Also, body heat tends to radiate to exposed concrete that is even a few degrees below the room temperature, making the room feel colder than it really is. The simple solution for this, however, is to cover the concrete floor with a material that does not absorb heat, such as carpeting. This is considerably cheaper and a great deal easier than building up a wood subfloor that still must be covered with finished flooring of some kind.

The only time a built-up wood floor makes sense in a basement is if the concrete is very rough or uneven, or if you want to change the floor level. But even then it is pointless to add insulation. Two inches of foamboard in the floor, for instance, will decrease your heating bills by less than ½ of 1% a year, so it would take a great many years just to recover the cost of the insulation.

Dampness

Before any kind of floor treatment is applied — paint, tile, wood or carpeting — check for dampness by laying a rubber mat down for two or three days or taping a square of polyethylene film to the concrete. If you see any sign of dampness when you remove these, steps must be taken to remedy this situation before proceeding (see Wet Basements, Page 18).

Paint

The cheapest and fastest way to finish the floor is to paint it. There are a number of good concrete floor paints on the market. Make certain the floor is clean, dry and free of any trace of oil or grease. The latter can be removed with one of the de-greasing compounds sold at hardware and auto supply stores.

Regardless of the type or brand of paint you are going to use, it's advisable to etch the concrete first with a solution of 1 part muriatic acid to 10 parts water, or the proportion recommended on the label. When it stops foaming, rinse off and allow to dry thoroughly before painting.

Tile

The only kind of resilient tile flooring that can be laid on concrete below grade is vinyl-asbestos. Tiles come in three thicknesses — $1/16''$, $.080''$, and $1/8''$. The .080 gauge is most commonly used; $1/16''$ is a little cheaper but more likely to show up any slight roughness or other surface imperfections in the concrete.

Easiest to lay are the relatively new peel-off, self-stick tiles (see photograph above). These only come in the $1/16''$ thickness. These are also the only kind of tile that is recommended for application on painted concrete.

Make sure the floor surface is clean, dry and smooth before you start. Pits, cracks and other irregularities in the concrete should be filled with one of the concrete patching materials available at all hardware and building supply stores.

Resist the temptation to start laying tile in one corner of the room working out. This can be done, but you're liable to end up with a narrow border that won't look very neat. Here's the proper way to do it:

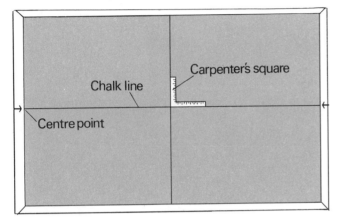

Mark the mid-point of the end walls, then snap a chalk line across the floor. Find the centre of this line and use a carpenter's square to mark a line at right-angles to it. Snap another chalk line along this across the room. You will now have divided the room into quarters.

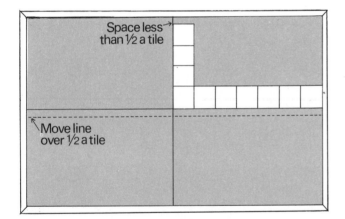

Lay a row of dry tiles from the centre point to one wall. If the space between the last tile and the wall is less than 4″, move the centre point either back or forward half a tile, then snap a new line through this point parallel to the first line. Repeat this procedure for the tiles going across the room in the other direction, again moving the centre line if necessary. You will now have located the centre lines to give you even borders more than half a tile wide around the room.

Starting at the centre point, lay the tiles in one quarter of the room at a time. Self-adhesive tiles need only be peeled and pressed in position. If tiles are being laid with adhesive, follow the manufacturer's instructions regarding the type of sealer, if any, and adhesive to use. Apply it right up to the chalk lines, but try not to cover them.

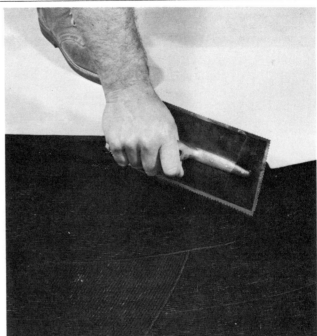

The adhesive should be spread with a notched trowel of the recommended size. If the notches are too shallow or too widely spaced, or if the trowel is held at too low an angle, not enough adhesive will be applied and the tile will not be properly bonded to the concrete. It's a good idea to check by laying a few tiles, pressing them in place, and then lifting one or two to see how much of the tile has been covered with adhesive. At least 50% of the underside of the tile should be covered.

Lay each tile down carefully and press it in place ... don't slide it. Notice the direction of the arrow on the back of each tile. If you are laying a patterned tile, the arrows should all point in the same direction. If you are using a marbled tile it's better to alternate the direction of each tile.

It's also important to press the tiles firmly in place after they have been laid. Professionals use a 150-pound linoleum roller, and you can rent one of these from any tool rental shop.

Border tiles can be cut with tin snips or heavy-duty scissors. There's an easy way to measure them. Lay a loose tile exactly on top of the last full tile, then put another tile on top of this one and slide it over to the wall. Using the edge of this top tile, mark the loose tile below it. Cut the tile along this mark and it will fit the border space exactly.

Floors

Carpeting

If a concrete floor is perfectly dry, any kind of carpeting can be laid on it. Often, however, a floor that seems to be dry may be slightly damp at some time of the year, either because of inadequate drainage during wet weather or because of condensation on a cool floor slab during hot, humid weather. (See Wet Basements, Page 18.)

Certain precautions should be taken, therefore, before laying carpet on concrete in order to avoid the possibility of mildew developing underneath it. There is less chance of dampness if the floor is painted or tiled. In areas where there is high humidity during the hot summer months, a dehumidifier should be used in the basement. And it is better to use a separate underlay of waffle-back sponge rubber or urethane foam than to buy a sponge-backed carpet that has no ventilation underneath.

Wall-to-wall carpeting can be laid on concrete just as easily as on a wood floor. "Smooth-edge," a narrow strip of wood with a slanting row of steel pins that grip the carpet backing, can be fastened to the floor around the perimeter of the room with special concrete nails or adhesive. The underlay fits inside the smooth-edge strip and the carpet is applied over them both. This job is best done by a professional, however.

Built-up Wood Floor

Although this is rarely required, as already discussed, if you do need a built-up floor, the best time to put it down is before the walls are framed. It can, however, be put in afterwards, but this is usually more difficult, particularly if there are partition walls.

First cover the floor with 4- or 6-mil polyethylene film or paint it with an asphalt sealer. These should extend up the foundation wall above the level of the finished floor. Next lay your floor supports, or sleepers, across the narrow width of the floor. If ceiling height is a problem, use 2x3 sleepers, but 2x4s are preferable and larger sizes can be used for higher floor levels. Cut back the ends of the sleepers as shown in the illustration above.

The sleepers are spaced 16" apart on centers by means of 14½" girts or blocking. These must be smaller than the sleepers so that there will be a space between the top of the girt and the plywood subfloor, as shown. Two-by-two girts will do for all sizes of sleepers. This provides ventilating space under the

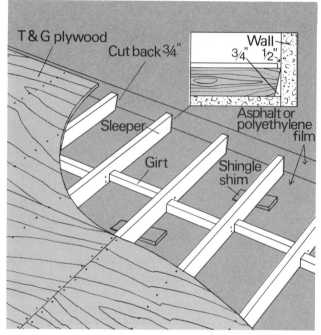

floor in order to reduce the possibility of moisture build-up and resulting wood decay, a common problem with built-up floors on concrete below ground level.

The girts should be staggered as shown to simplify nailing. It isn't necessary to fasten the girts or the sleepers to the concrete. The floor platform will stay solidly in place by its own weight.

Subflooring

Five-eights or ¾" tongue-and-groove plywood is nailed to the sleepers with 1¼" or 1½" ringed flooring nails spaced every 6" along the sleepers. The tongue-and-groove plywood does not require support under the panel joints and need only be nailed there if the joint falls on a sleeper. Tongue-and-groove panels do not butt tightly together, but should have a gap of about 1/32", the thickness of a paper matchbook cover.

To avoid continuous panel joints across the room, start in a corner with a full panel, then place a half-panel beside it. Alternate full and half panels this way across the room to stagger the end joints.

Don't butt the panels tight to the walls, however. Place them about ½" away, leaving a gap for the circulation of air under the floor. This gap will be hidden, but not blocked, by the baseboard, which should be placed about ¼" above the level of the finished floor.

Carpeting, tiles, sheet-vinyl, or hardwood flooring can be laid on top of the plywood subfloor.

17 Soundproofing

With its concrete floor and walls, a basement is built like an echo chamber that reflects and amplifies sound waves. Recreational sounds from the basement can keep the upstairs living room jumping. Or music and talking upstairs may seem to be in the same room with someone trying to read, relax or sleep in the rec room.

The common ceiling/floor may seem like the best place to start soundproofing, but the most effective and practical approach to the problem is to absorb the troublesome sounds at their source.

Sound bounces off smooth, hard surfaces but is scattered and dispersed by rough ones. Soft, porous materials soak up sound like a sponge. One of the best ways to reduce noise levels in the basement is to put deep pile carpet on the concrete floor. Acoustic tiles on the ceiling will also help to absorb sounds before they go upstairs. Such tiles have a perforated or fissured surface that may look merely decorative, but is scientifically designed to catch sound waves of various frequencies.

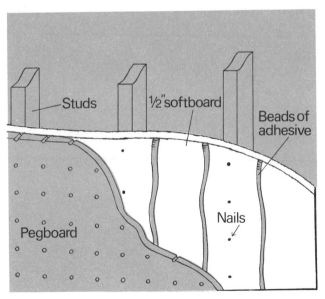

Burlap fabric, textured paint, or porous, rough-textured materials like cork can be applied to the walls to absorb or scatter sounds. An inexpensive and very effective soundproofing material for the wall can be made by covering ½" softboard paneling with perforated pegboard, fastened with panel adhesive. The pegboard can be painted, but use a roller so that the paint won't fill the holes and prevent them from absorbing the sound waves.

The trick in building a soundproof ceiling is to isolate it from the floor joists and other structural members as much as possible. A suspended ceiling (see Page 78) makes a better sound barrier than one that is fastened directly to the joists.

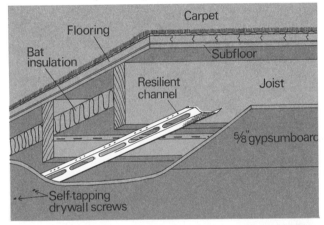

But weight plays a large part in sound absorption, and a heavy material like gypsumboard can be more effective than the conventional, lightweight softboard ceiling panels if applied so that it is isolated from the ceiling structure. This can be done by fastening the panels to the joists by means of resilient metal channel strips that are designed to absorb sound vibrations and prevent them reaching the framework of the floor above.

A further reduction in the transmission of airborne sounds through the ceiling is achieved by placing 3½" friction-fit fibreglass insulation batts between the joists. The batts should not be pushed up tight to the floor, however. If necessary, 15" lengths of coathanger wire can be shoved up between the joists to support the batts.

Sound leaks through holes like water through a basket, so great care must be taken to block off any openings made in the ceiling for lighting fixtures or heating outlets. This can best be done by packing them with fibreglass batts.

Acoustic ceiling tiles can be applied to the gypsumboard with dabs of mastic adhesive, or the panels joints can be taped and filled (see Page 69) and the ceiling painted.

18 Coping a Mitre

Mouldings are used in many places when you are finishing a basement, around the ceiling and baseboard, door and window trim, counter edging, and built-in furniture. This requires a lot of inside and outside miter joints, which can lead to a lot of mistakes if you're not sure what you're doing. Cutting one miter the wrong way, for instance, can waste a whole length of moulding.

Miter cuts on some kinds of mouldings are obvious and easy, but more complicated moulding, such as cove and crown, is often mis-cut by being put in the miter box the wrong way. A few carpentry tricks and the right tools will save you a lot of trouble and un-necessary expense.

You need a miter box and a back saw to cut regular 45° miters, and a coping saw to make the 90° coped joints that experts use to make tight-fitting inside corners around the ceiling and baseboard, as shown in the accompanying photographs.

With a coped joint, one piece of moulding is simply square-cut the length of the wall to fit snugly in the corner. The other piece of moulding (usually the shorter wall) is coped as shown. A coped joint is much easier to fit and makes a neater joint. Only inside corners can be coped; outside corners must be mitered in the usual way with two 45° cuts.

1. The first step in making a coped miter joint is to square-cut and fasten one length of moulding along the feature wall of the room, usually the one facing you as you enter. It is shown here on the right. Hold the other piece so you can see how the miter is to be cut.

3. Place the moulding in your miter box, using the pencil mark to line up the 45° cut. (If this is not done it's very easy to become confused and cut the miter the wrong way.) The simple wooden miter box with metal guides shown here is adequate for cutting mouldings.

2. Turn the moulding down and mark the approximate angle of the miter cut on the top of the moulding.

4. Now use a coping saw to cut away the mitered wood, following the edge of the miter cut as a guide.

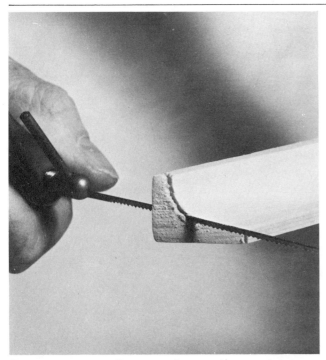

5. With the moulding turned over, the remaining excess wood is cut off with the coping saw, still following the edge of the miter.

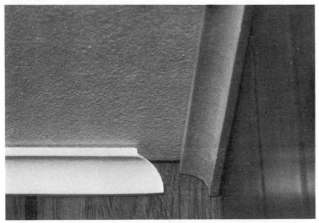

6. The coped moulding, on the left, will now fit snugly over the curved face of the first piece of moulding, making a tight joint that looks like a conventional miter joint.

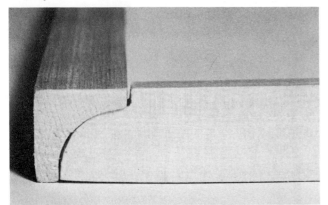

7. The same joint, viewed from the back, shows how the coped moulding on the right has been cut to fit.

Here is the right way to put a piece of crown or cove moulding in the miter box. Beginners usually make the mistake of placing the large, flat face on the back of the moulding against the side of the miter box. That will not make a proper miter cut.

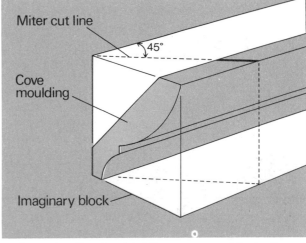

If you visualize the moulding as a square block of wood you will see why it must be placed in the miter box as shown in the illustration above.

After the miter cut has been made and the projecting wood has been cut off with a coping saw as shown in the previous photographs, this is the way the coped joint will fit in the corner. Baseboard moulding is treated the same manner.

19 Bars and Other Built-Ins

Your finished basement living areas will be a lot more useful if you include such built-ins as a bar counter, bookshelves, seating, bunk beds and storage cabinets for such things as games and hobby equipment. Extra storage is very important, because you will have lost a lot of the open storage space you had in the unfinished basement. Maybe it was messy, but it did hold a number of things that must now be accommodated elsewhere.

So make use of every bit of space you have for miscellaneous storage. Basement walls generally have to weave and jog around obstructions like posts, pipes, stairways, laundry tubs, furnace, oil tank, etc., and it is often possible to use the resulting alcoves and wall projections for built-ins of various kinds. This may require no more work than closing in the front of an alcove with sliding doors; the other three sides of the enclosed space will be already finished. Enclosures like this also make the room look much neater because they eliminate awkward projections.

Here an alcove 4' deep and 6½' long has provided space for a built-in chesterfield-daybed and a hidden upper bunk. The matresses are supported by ribbon springs and there is drawer space under the lower unit for the storage of blankets and linen. When it is not needed, the upper bunk is concealed by triple-track sliding doors. Pipe brackets are used as a ladder to the top bunk (and as a magazine rack). A 24" fluorescent tube, recessed under the head of the top bunk, illuminates the chesterfield corner.

Another good example of how an awkward projection can be put to practical use is this attractive bookcase unit that also conceals the electrical service panel. After the wall was panelled around the service boxes, a shelf ladder was constructed out of 1x8 lumber to fit the opening and fastened to the wall. A 1x3 header across the top provides additional support, and 1x2 strips nailed to the edge of the uprights improve the appearance and provide a hinge support for the plywood doors that provide access to the service panel.

A split-level floor plan and a reverse stairway that cut into the end of a narrow recreation room created a difficult corner in the basement remodelling project shown in the before-and-after photographs on this page. It was also necessary to retain access to the crawlspace storage area under the landing.

The solution was to build an L-shaped bar counter into the corner, creating an attractive landing at the entrance to the room. The counter section under the upper stair projection is hinged to provide access to the bar, behind which there is an opening into the crawlspace storage area.

A lowered ceiling section over the counter is fitted with recessed lights to illuminate the counter. The bar is faced with the same barnboard panelling used on the walls. Construction details of this bar counter are given on the following pages.

Bars and Other Built-Ins

The bar counter is made out of ¾″ plywood plus a few pieces of 1x2 for shelf supports and counter edging. The vertical partitions are 42″ high and 18″ deep, with a notch 3″ deep and 4″ high in the bottom for the kick space. Shelves are nailed to the partition on one side, to a 1x2 nailing strip on the other, a very simple system that requires the minimum of cabinet work. The size and position of the bar can best be checked by drawing it on the floor with a carpenter's crayon.

Details of the construction of the ceiling soffit over the bar can be seen in these two photographs. The inside dimension of the soffit is outlined with 1x3 nailing strips fastened to the ceiling joists, then the 1x6 sides of the soffit are nailed to these. A ladder of 1x3s nailed between the sides provides reinforcement and also supports the retaining rings for the lighting fixtures.

The ceiling tiles are then applied to the underside of the soffit, being careful to keep them in line with the tile pattern on the main ceiling. The sides of the soffit are covered with the same panelling used on the walls.

Because the main beam and its supporting posts are usually located down the centre of the basement — and the furnace, hot water tank, and laundry tubs are generally all on one side — the space available for finished living area in a basement is generally long and narrow.

A convenient way to divide this space into separate activity areas is by the construction of a storage wall unit designed to serve the rooms on both sides. In the example shown here, the main area is a hobby and music room, with a bedroom at the far end. The two rooms are separated by a storage wall 3' thick.

On the hobby room side (above) the partition wall is used for bookshelves, stereo components and a large library of record albums. The bookshelves are adjustable. The fixed record shelves are divided into sections by vertical partitions.

On the bedroom side (right) the deep storage wall provides generous wardrobe space concealed behind sliding doors. The bedroom itself can be closed off from the hobby room with a "pocket" door that slides into the storage wall on the right, where there is additional wardrobe space.

20 Installing a Fireplace

Whether or not you need it for auxiliary heat, a fireplace is a very desirable addition to a basement living area. If you are fortunate enough to have a roughed-in fireplace already, completing it will present no problem. The face can be finished with tile, brick, stone, stucco, or any other non-combustible material.

But even if you don't have a roughed-in opening and a spare chimney flue, it's still possible to put a real fireplace in your basement. You can now buy prefabricated metal fireplaces and insulated, stainless-steel chimneys that are much cheaper and easier to install than conventional fireplaces. The metal fireplaces come in free-standing models as well as "zero clearance" models that can be built into a wood frame wall.

For basement installation, the metal chimney from the fireplace can go out through a hole in the top of the foundation wall and continue up the outside wall to the roof, supported only by the existing framework of the house.

Concrete block supports are placed and levelled to raise the fireplace to the desired height above the basement floor. A wood foundation can be used, however, because the outside shell of the metal fireplace never gets hot and does not need a fireproof support. The basement walls have already been panelled to the edge of the fireplace area.

The corner fireplace shown here is one of many different styles that can be built using the sheet-metal units. The impressive brick face and chimney are actually just a brick veneer applied to a plywood frame constructed around the sheet-metal shell and installed as shown in the following photographs.

Zero clearance units that can be installed in the centre of the wall are also available.

A 12" hole is knocked through the concrete block wall to accommodate the T-shaped fitting for the metal chimney. This connects with another T supported on a bracket on the outside wall. Typical chimney installation details are shown in the drawing on the right. Local regulations on the installation and use of metal fireplaces vary. Check with your building department.

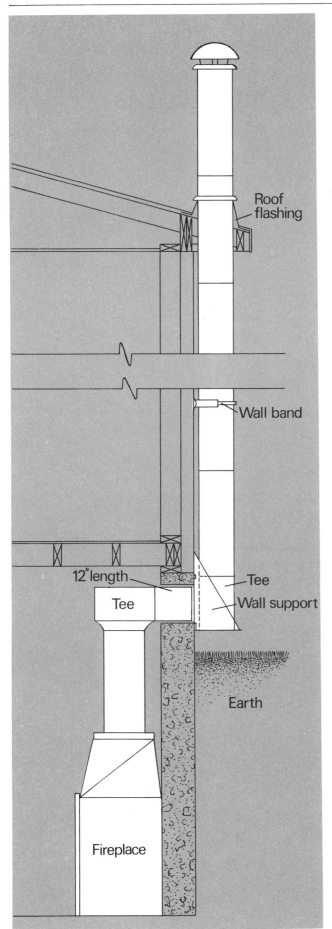

Roof flashing

Wall band

12" length

Tee

Tee

Wall support

Earth

Fireplace

A free-standing fireplace, such as this Franklin-style model, should be placed on a fireproof base of brick, concrete or stone. In this case, the raised plywood platform is faced with thin stone veneer, as is the panel behind the fireplace. Since the foundation wall happens to be entirely below ground level, the chimney pipe goes through the wall to the T-connection shown below and then extends up through the roof overhang.

Photography Credits

Ken Ingham — Page 72
John Mitchell — Pages 10, 11, 13-15, 19-21, 26-29, 32, 35-43, 45, 46, 53, 57, 60-71, 75-79, 84, 85, 88, 91
Ian Samson — Pages 22, 72
Clive Weber — Page 89

Aikenhead Hardware — Page 25
Armstrong Cork — Pages 80, 81
Bondex International — Page 12
Canadian Gypsum Company — Page 59
Canadian Portland Cement Association — Page 12
Lansing-Buildall — Pages 69, 79, 86
Masonite Canada — Pages 50, 51
Morval-Durofoam — Pages 30, 31
Thorosystem Products — Pages 16, 17
Weldwood Canada — Page 51

We would like to thank the following firms and organizations for their assistance in the preparation of this book:

Aikenhead Hardware Ltd.
Armstrong Cork Industries Ltd.
Bondex International (Canada) Ltd.
Canadian Carpet Institute
Canadian Gypsum Company Ltd.
Canadian Portland Cement Association
Canfor Ltd.
Central Mortgage & Housing Corporation
Council of Forest Industries of British Columbia (COFI)
Dominion Foundries and Steel Ltd. (DOFASCO)
Domtar Ltd.
Fibreglass Canada Ltd.
Lansing-Buildall
Masonite Canada Ltd.
Morval-Durofoam Ltd.
Ontario Hydro
Ramset Ltd.
Selkirk-Metalbestos Ltd.
Steel Company of Canada Ltd. (STELCO)
Thorosystem Products of Canada Ltd.
Weldwood of Canada Sales Ltd.

Index

Index